The Best Outcomes for Young People

Dedication

To Richard and Declan, you have been the wind beneath my wings x

Acknowledgements

I have had the most fabulous career and met so many inspirational people on the way. I learnt early in my career what kind of teacher I did not want to be. To Mr Smith, my form teacher, who told my mum I would be lucky to get a job in Woolworths: you gave me the determination to reach my dreams of being a home economics teacher and that if you believe in yourself, it doesn't matter where you come from. I came from a mining village in Yorkshire and ended up being honoured by the Queen; I said to my late brother, '*How does a lass from "Cas" get to the palace?*' to which he responded, '*The lass from "Cas" worked hard*' and helped me throw off my imposter syndrome.

To every member of staff who has worked for me and helped implement my aspirations of what we can do for those vulnerable pupils that schools had given up on. Especially Diane, my PA, who made every day doable and to those headteachers who had confidence in me and supported my ideals.

I would particularly like to thank the following who have gone over and above to support me in writing this book: Stella Hulley for her belief in me, patience, support and reading of every chapter; Alison Waters for her insight; Margaret McCann for her constant encouragement; Dr Karl Huntbach for his support and for reaffirming why love matters when working with vulnerable pupils; and to Cath Kitchen, Bryony Cook, Joe Barker and the Jigsaw team for their contributions. To my ex-pupils and parents who were brave enough to share their story in the final chapter, thank you.

Of course, nothing is possible without the love and support of your family: Ric, Dec, Emily and Terry never stopped believing in me. To my friends who were always there to pour a cup of tea or glass of wine and just listen throughout my career. And last but not least to every pupil who has had the misfortune of being in my care. I hope you have forgiven me for the tough love I provided but know that I never stopped believing in your ability to succeed and most of all your right to be happy.

Janice Cahill, OBE

The Best Outcomes for Young People

Lessons from a PRU Headteacher

Janice Cahill

Routledge
Taylor & Francis Group

LONDON AND NEW YORK

First published in 2024 by Critical Publishing Ltd

Published 2025 by Routledge
4 Park Square, Milton Park, Abingdon, Oxon OX14 4RN
605 Third Avenue, New York, NY 10017

Routledge is an imprint of the Taylor & Francis Group, an informa business

British Library Cataloguing in Publication Data
A CIP record for this book is available from the British Library

ISBN: 9781915713605 (pbk)
ISBN: 9781041057444 (ebk)

The right of Janice Cahill to be identified as the Author of this work has been asserted by her in accordance with the Copyright, Design and Patents Act 1988.

Text design by Greensplash
Cover design by Out of House Limited

DOI: 10.4324/9781041057444

Contents

About the author

Janice Cahill OBE has been in education for 42 years and remains passionate about supporting children and young people with social, emotional and mental health (SEMH) needs. She has set up a range of services, including a mental health team that works in mainstream schools, and was instrumental in providing the foundation for mental health services and education working more closely together. She has contributed to many local and national initiatives about SEMH and has been a guest speaker at several conferences. She was awarded an OBE in 2019 for her work with vulnerable children and mental health services.

1 Social, emotional and mental health (SEMH) is not rocket science

Survival skills

Life is hard, as many of us know. My job as a headteacher of a pupil referral unit (PRU) was to teach as many survival skills as I could to the most vulnerable children referred to my unit to make sure that when they left my small educational provision, they could survive in the much bigger school or work environment. The many facets of children can be seen or heard in a PRU or alternative provision (AP), a microcosm of society, and each unique individual needs these survival skills so they can take their rightful place in society.

The next time you go into your school hall, stand, watch and listen. If you take a minute to observe, a thousand things will expose themselves:

- the abused child;
- the angry child;
- the emotionally fragile child;
- the frightened child;
- the child just wanting to be a child.

These children, whose lives have often been turned upside down, their emotions erased at such a young age by the viciousness of society and by their own interpretations and perceptions of their own self-worth, need our support.

Several years ago, I asked every member of my team to write 500 words on what it meant to them to work in a PRU. They shared their thoughts through poetry, rap tunes, recipes and visually through art. It was quite an eye-opener and a compelling read for everyone with all their musings brought together in a book. Here is my contribution.

How should you ready yourselves for your pupils each day?

1. *The geese are flying low – our call of danger but if you look closely, you will see that their flight path is not very far from our heads.*

2. *The monkey walk – bottoms out, chest out, their whole bodies stiff with anxiety and we begin to say 'be aware'.*

3. *Shifting sands – what was once the exceptional becomes the norm but we must never let their norm become ours or we are in danger of failing them.*

4. *Talk to the hand – they're not being rude, it's just their way of coping.*

5. *What doesn't kill you makes you stronger! – we learn every day.*

6. *Smile – with sincerity.*

7. *Doh! – not one of us is perfect and remember it's okay to not know the answer.*

But the biggest thing we have to teach our children is acceptance – of whom they are, a unique individual and of where they have been – to help them turn their faces to the sun away from the dark side and to learn to love themselves.

And what characterises the staff?

They need to be and are exceptional, to be able to give lots of TLC and respect, and an understanding that sometimes it's just too hard to be in the child's world. A sense of humour is essential but a belief that every child is born good is the mantra.

- Is this job hard? Absolutely
- Where else would I rather be? Nowhere
- Am I the luckiest person alive – of course!

Introduction to the work of a PRU and AP

My journey

I was humbled to be the headteacher of a PRU for 25 years. It was quite a journey and I have been asked by many people if I could write down what were the strengths of the unit, which achieved outstanding outcomes, and how this could be mirrored in other areas. My response has always been that this is not 'rocket science' and my work has primarily been based on the simple principles of building human relationships and kindness. After being a teacher and a headteacher for 42 years, I feel I have experiences and stories to share about how you should engage with your pupils to enable them to grow as independent and happy young people.

On leaving college I worked in mainstream education as a home economics teacher; by default, I began working as an outreach teacher for a PRU. This entailed me working in local secondary schools with pupils who for a vast array of reasons were finding school difficult. I worked closely with heads of year, deputy heads, education welfare officers and educational psychologists. Our role was to work out what was going wrong and to try and keep them in education, preferably in their existing mainstream school. If after assessment we felt the pupil needed time out, they were then transferred to the PRU. In effect, I was the 'gatekeeper'.

In those days the PRU was the receiver of any child who either couldn't or wouldn't go to school. We taught permanently excluded pupils alongside pupils who were too anxious to attend school and those with extreme medical conditions. We would teach some pupils in their home who could not come out of their bedrooms, and they received three hours of education each week. In 1995, those attending the PRU were entitled to 12 hours of education each week, so we had a morning group and an afternoon group. We taught English, maths, science, food technology and art. We had no specialist rooms and staff had to be imaginative with minimal resources but it was those early days that helped me to set up the service that I left 25 years later – one that ensured every pupil accessed a minimum of 25 hours of education each week, with a curriculum that equalled the quality of that provided within a mainstream school. Every pupil had the opportunity to achieve GCSEs and other accredited qualifications alongside attendance at their mainstream schools; I talk about reintegration in Chapter 6.

Working with families

For many of the families I have met, their relationship with their child's mainstream school had broken down – this is not about apportioning blame or saying mainstream schools got it wrong, but the environment and their child's needs needed a little bit more. Mainstream schools are very busy places. From my experience and the secondary headteachers I have had the privilege to work with, they do an amazing job but it is often external demands that guide their actions. Ofsted is just one of these, and the moral dilemmas this raises often guides what is the next best step for them to do with pupils displaying social, emotional and mental health (SEMH) difficulties.

In my opinion, PRUs start at a disadvantage. The guidance on provision is fairly sketchy – look around the country or ask a colleague and you will both share a range of provisions and it is difficult to find a comparable one you can benchmark against. Everything you do is open to national, regional and local interpretation. The PRU cohort are the young people that schools have worked hard with but within the demands of that environment those children and young people have not succeeded.

However, the AP population is made up of a greater number of pupils than those who are just permanently excluded. Data collection is very difficult, especially due to Covid-19, but the approximate numbers based on 2019 data show that there are currently 421 PRUs in England and there are approximately 16,000 pupils who attend PRUs, AP academies or free schools and other provision like further education (FE) colleges. This doesn't include a further 9897 pupils who also attend alternative APs but have a mainstream school as the main school at which they are registered. There are also 22,848 pupils educated in other forms of APs, which includes, but is not exclusive to, independent schools and providers that are not able to register as a school.

If these provisions are not closely monitored, then the quality of education the most vulnerable pupils in our society receive could be judged as second class, and from my perspective this is not acceptable.

The need for PRUs and APs

Being a teenager is not easy. We often hear this missive as if it is a kind of excuse for poor behaviour and wrong choices. But whichever era we were born into, the teenage years are often filled with angst, both emotionally and academically. Very few people understand the mechanisms of their hormonal growth and the feelings and emotions that are stirred up. Every generation can recall how bad it was in their youth and how their parents did things differently. As we become parents, we also recall what we did, why we did it and the impact it had on our children.

For some pupils, time out of their mainstream education is needed. This should never be seen as a permanent option or solution. PRUs and APs should be seen as the continuum of the educational offer, not outside it and definitely not as a punishment. They should be seen as that 'step out' and 'step in' offer working in partnership with mainstream schools. Some educationalists would challenge this belief as they believe that PRUs and APs should not exist as schools should be able to facilitate and support their needs. But I believe that for some pupils they need to step out of their school environment and have time for reflection and support and to receive effective interventions.

Unfortunately, PRUs do not get a good press. This is often based on scaremongering shared through public media which tells of the extreme behaviours and the poor quality of education they provide. However, this can be challenged in many ways. I would be the first to advocate the impact of and the need for PRUs, not as an alternative to mainstream but as an equal and effective partner.

Covid-19 and its legacy

We have never before experienced the scale of disruption to our lives as that experienced during the global Covid-19 pandemic. Like with all difficulties, some children will bounce back while others will need more support. However, the scale of the impact of this trauma on both young people's and adults' well-being and mental health has been significant and schools are still coming to terms with its impact and the continuing need to support pupils who have found it difficult to return or as yet have still to walk through the school doors. Schools have been creative in developing programmes of work to facilitate the return to school and to support the needs of the whole school community in their transition back into routine, expectations and academic learning. The data which is currently being shared through the National Centre for Social Research (2022) states that:

- pre-pandemic, one in nine pupils had a mental health difficulty;
- in 2020, one in six pupils had a mental health difficulty;
- in 2023, this had risen to one in four.

This data is for all age groups, Key Stage 1–4, with the Key Stage 4 group being more heavily weighted, and it shares a challenging message for those working with pupils.

REFLECTIVE TASK

- Thinking about the school you work in, how do you identify with this data and what changes have you had to put in place to support the learner who is finding it difficult to return to school?
- What options are there available in your local authority to support this process?

The difference between a PRU, AP and special school

It is often very difficult to clearly distinguish between a PRU and AP. After all these years, there is still confusion and every local authority will interpret these categories to fit the needs of their pupils and those of their authority. Every government I have worked with in my years as a headteacher appeared to struggle to provide clear guidance on what is a PRU and what is an AP. They leave every aspect of the character of the provision to each local authority so that interpretation is very difficult to navigate. Ultimately, pupils can be placed in PRUs and APs incorrectly and for long periods of time. If you ask any search engine for the definition you will not get a clear answer and ultimately become more confused. The definitions I have written below are based on my understanding.

Pupil referral units

These are often known as PRUs and are local authority provisions that cater for children who are unable to attend a mainstream school for numerous reasons, including non-attendance, behavioural difficulties, illness and being assessed in relation to their special educational needs. They are not a school; they are a *short-term* provision. Pupils should spend their time being assessed and have the opportunity to address their issues and return to their referring mainstream school or, if necessary, another school should be agreed and that return should be within a specific time frame. This time frame should not be years, but preferably up to six months and in some cases 12 months. There is no legal curricular framework but good practice promotes the teaching of English, maths and science. There are no clear building expectations and no requirements for specific teaching areas or support areas.

Alternative provisions

These provisions, known as APs, can be seen as both a short- and long-term placement and can be the permanent school for a pupil for an indefinite time, usually those that have been permanently excluded. APs are sometimes used for pupils who may have an education, health and care plan (EHCP) and this is potentially where issues can arise around the quality of the educational offer they may receive due to the simple fact that they are not a 'school'. There are no legal curricular guidelines, but again some teaching of English, maths and science is expected. There is no clarity on what the building should have to support the teaching and learning of the pupils who attend. This allows many APs to develop their own curriculum, which can be based on a more vocational/practical offer for pupils placed there.

Special schools

These are schools that cater specifically for pupils whose needs cannot be met with the provision and support provided by a mainstream school. Pupils generally need to have an EHCP to attend. There are clear curriculum guidelines and all special schools have to provide subject-specific classrooms and support areas.

According to the AP census 2022 (Gov.uk, 2022), which includes both PRUs and APs, an AP can fall into the following categories:

1. independent school;

2. hospital;

3. non-maintained special school;

4. not a school (ie FE college, one-to-one tuition, other registered provider, or work-based placement).

REFLECTIVE TASK

- In your local authority, what are the differences between a PRU, AP and special school?

- What do these provisions mean for the pupils you currently teach and why would you make a referral to them?

Legislation guiding PRUs and APs

The legislation and much of the guidance provided by the government is outdated and very unclear for the reader and implementer of this kind of educational provision. Many APs have been allowed to set up with little guidance and accountability, and unfortunately some schools have used them to 'fix' a problem. Whether or not this was right for the individual pupil is unclear, but it was right for the school at that moment to remove the pupil from their peers. It often feels that the decision has been made by headteachers with little understanding of the pupil's needs, and it can appear quite a punitive decision. I know of one pupil who went to a stable every day because they liked horses, but where is the education value in this placement? APs are also being used by local authorities to place pupils with an EHCP as they have no specialist school placements available.

I have highlighted the following documents which I think will help you establish some understanding of current government direction.

Alternative Provision: Statutory Guidance for Local Authorities, 2016

This document from the Department for Education (DfE, 2016a) explained the statutory powers and duties applicable to APs, the main points being as follows.

> *For the purposes of this guidance, the definition of alternative provision is as follows: education arranged by local authorities for pupils who, because of exclusion, illness or other reasons, would not otherwise receive suitable education; education arranged by schools for pupils on a fixed period exclusion; and pupils being directed by schools to off-site provision to improve their behaviour.*
>
> (DfE, 2016a, p 3)

The guidance clarified that a PRU can only be established by a local authority but only after they have explored the possibility of opening an AP academy. Any other school, trust or group of individuals can establish AP academies and AP free schools. Included in the guidance are issues around funding, management of the provision and a school's power to direct a pupil off site for education to improve their behaviour. While this is helpful, the perception of the word 'behaviour' can have negative connotations.

Timpson Review of School Exclusion, 2019

The purpose of the review was to look at exclusions and the reasons why they are used. This was a very thorough review and gave 30 main recommendations for the government, local authorities and schools to consider. There was a clear recognition that no teacher starts their career other than to help all children reach their potential. However, the review did find that in 2017, 0.1 per cent of the 8 million children in schools in England were permanently excluded, which equated to 40 children receiving a permanent exclusion every day. On top of this, 2000 pupils received a suspension for a fixed period every day.

The main points, summarised from the Department for Education (DfE, 2019), were as follows.

- Schools should be responsible for the children they exclude and accountable for their educational outcomes.

- The Department for Education (DfE) should update its statutory guidance on exclusion to provide more clarity on the use of exclusion.

- Ofsted should recognise schools who use exclusion appropriately and effectively.

- Training on behaviour and mental health should be a mandatory part of initial teacher training, as highlighted in the Carter Review of teacher training in 2015, and should be embedded into the Early Years Framework.

- The DfE should ensure that funding following an exclusion does not act as an incentive for schools to permanently exclude or discourage from admitting those pupils who have been excluded from another school.

- If a pupil receives multiple suspensions, they should not be left without being able to access education and the number of days the suspension is for should be reviewed. APs and PRUs within each authority should be consulted to determine whether they can admit the pupil to the provision or provide the necessary educational support.

- When a pupil moves to another school, AP or PRU, they should be systematically tracked to ensure they do not become lost in the system.

SEND and AP Improvement Plan: Right Support, Right Place, Right Time, 2023

In the most recent guidance titled *Special Educational Needs and Disabilities (SEND) and Alternative Provision (AP) Improvement Plan: Right Support, Right Place, Right Time*, the government state that local authorities should be able to identify support for those pupils who cannot attend their mainstream or special school.

> *Education arranged by local authorities for pupils who, because of exclusion, illness or other reasons, would not otherwise receive suitable education; education arranged by schools for pupils on a fixed period exclusion; and pupils being directed by schools to off-site provision to improve their behaviour.*

> *Types of AP providers include: AP academies, AP free schools, pupil referral units (PRUs), hospital schools, independent providers, further education colleges, and voluntary sector providers.*

> (DfE, 2013, p 3)

Clarity on the role of an AP or PRU has now been built into a three-tier model which helps with the planning and allocation of resources.

Tier 1 **Targeted support in mainstream schools** AP specialist early interventions and support to help at-risk pupils stay in mainstream school	**Tier 2** **Time-limited placements** Short-term placements in AP schools to assess and address pupils' needs, with the expectation of return to their mainstream school	**Tier 3** **Transitional placements** Placements in AP school for pupils who need support to move on to a new mainstream school or sustained post-16 destination

Effective reforms would move the system's emphasis upstream, away from expensive long-term placements

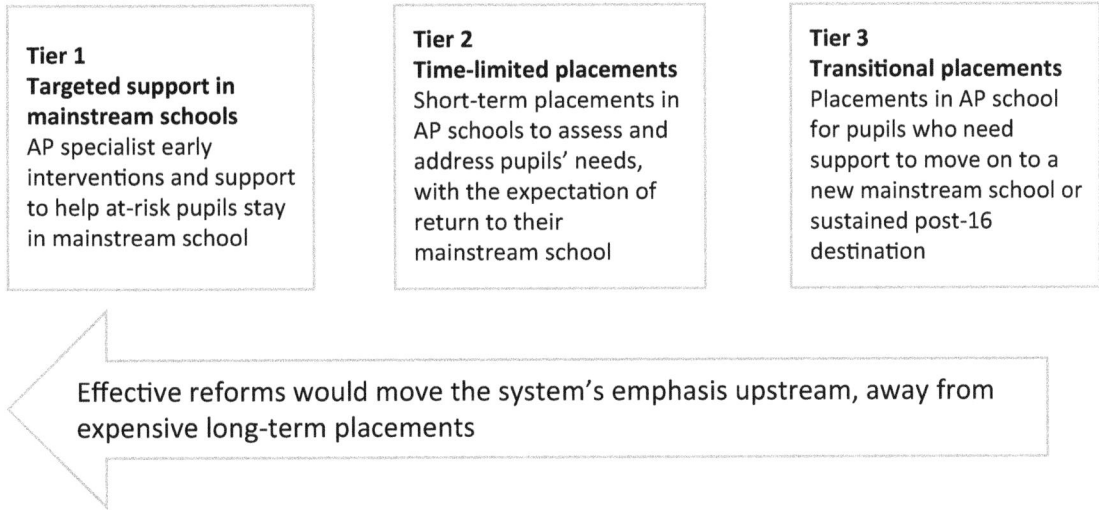

Figure 1.1 *A three-tier model for alternative provision*

REFLECTIVE TASK

- Look at Figure 1.1; what word has now been used to describe an AP? Does this cloud your understanding?

Types of PRUs and APs

As shared previously, there are many kinds of PRUs and APs but they generally cater for:

- pregnant schoolgirls;
- excluded pupils;
- SEMH pupils;
- pupils with diagnosed mental health difficulties.

They can also include hospital schools.

However, this is not a definitive list and many other needs can be included.

What makes a good PRU or AP?

Like any successful recipe, there are ingredients which ensure the success of a dish. Using this analogy, you must also have a vision of what the end product will look like for your PRU. The transition from an idea to a more detailed plan must show why the provision is different from anything else available and how it will work. You need to bring together a group of people who sign up collectively to the 'idea' and are willing to take on a collective ownership of how the idea can be put into practice and the impact it will have on the pupils you admit.

As the provision is developed, more expertise can be added so that staff have a range of skills and have the competencies to face the challenges that will be presented. Staff need to have a collective vision of what needs to be done and how they will contribute to the success. To continue the analogy, if the ingredients are right and they 'blend' together the provision has a chance of being successful. I also believe that the provision needs to be self-reliant and will not fail just because one person leaves, but will continue to thrive and be successful. Staff need to be adaptable and ready to change not so much the core structure but their approach to teaching and learning.

The provision needs to have a clear mission statement defining what you are about, what the provision stands for and what it expects of each member of staff to ensure the provision's primary objectives are met. This cultural identity will not only make it easier to get the best from all the staff who work in the provision but it allows the staff to acknowledge and work within the boundaries established.

CASE STUDY

This was my ethos in a nutshell:

Social exclusion or rejection is not simply one misfortune among many, nor just a bit of sad drama – it strikes at the heart of what our psyche is designed for.

(Baumeister, 2005, p 1)

Everyone needs to feel they belong and to feel that their contribution is valued. The success of the provision I led was in part the result of the cultural legacy established by its initial six members of staff. We knew that there would be both personal and professional challenges but we also knew that we were never on our own and were there for each other as a team.

To succeed I had to bring together a team who had experience of working within the mainstream school environment and understood the pressures that colleagues faced within those establishments. We also knew that we had to get people to go beyond working together; they had to work for each other. Everyone had to feel that their input would contribute to the whole, that the 'them' and 'us' culture could not exist, and they knew we would succeed or fail together. We all had an important job to do, and no one individual was more important than anyone else.

However, establishing our culture took more than one person to make it work. All new staff were inducted into our 'culture' to ensure that the progress we were making was not only continued but strengthened through their contribution. Each person was responsible for their own actions and achievements, but they also had to be prepared to feel a collective responsibility for the actions and achievements of their colleagues. If someone was slipping behind in their work, what could we do to help them out? Was there a better way to achieve a particular outcome? If you got something wrong, you needed to understand the impact that had on your colleagues. Every staff member was invested in not only doing their best, but in getting the best from each other. This approach was the antithesis of many other APs where individual attainment was built on a 'survival of the fittest' mentality that was valued above the kind of shared ownership and collective responsibility model that characterises the way we developed.

People were chosen to join the provision because their character 'fit' our culture, not just because they had the right skills. When I interviewed for staff, the last question I gave to everyone was the following.

Tell me in 30 words why I should employ you?

I have to say this question did not make me popular, as I counted every word and stopped them when the 30 words was reached but it helped me to find out what their passion was, if it would fit in and how they would complement our existing team.

If a provision can be said to have a personality, then we did, and this was reflected very strongly by the people that worked there. After our first inspection I was asked what made us special – my response was that it was like 'magic' and you can imagine the responses I got from that one! Our ambition has been that all staff buy into the ethos which is based on good values of decency, honesty, respect and hard work, and to build a PRU that would show how you could make a difference to the lives of many vulnerable students. A sense of humour was also essential.

In effect, my dream became everyone's dream and to get the job done, the early team understood that they needed to be prepared to make sacrifices. I stressed that every job across the centre was important to its overarching success; everyone has a job to do, and they must do it as best as they could. Every member of staff worked in each of the specialist areas as they evolved so that they understood what that job entailed and so that they could make a valuable contribution to its development. All staff spent at least three days in mainstream school every year, shadowing a colleague within their subject area, and had to teach a lesson to 30 pupils so they could understand the reality of mainstream school teaching. This enhanced their teaching within the provision.

Ultimately, the success I achieved was through a collective undertaking by a diverse group of gifted individuals, united by a common 'culture' which had the sole aim to design, build and create a pupil referral unit that interfaced with mainstream schools to support inclusion and provide our students with the best of both worlds.

Developing a good PRU or AP

In my opinion, the following are needed in order to develop a good PRU/AP:

- staff who have taught for at least three years in a mainstream school setting;
- a vision of a curriculum that is equal to that in a mainstream school;
- a clear vision and purpose;
- effective and strong partnerships with your mainstream schools.

In the document *Educational Excellence Everywhere* (DfE, 2016b), it was found that while some provisions were outstanding, you could often see:

a) *pupils in AP whose specific needs would be better addressed in a main-stream school;*

b) *pupils entering AP without an agreed plan for their educational success;*

c) *teachers without the knowledge and skills expected in mainstream schools;*

d) *weak lines of accountability for commissioners and providers;*

e) *the most challenging pupils being placed with the weakest providers;*

f) *those leaving AP struggling to find post-16 provision that helps them to continue their progress.*

(DfE, 2016b, p 102)

All the above highlighted the areas we had in effect considered and hopefully 'got right'. But there was never a sense of complacency as our pupils and their needs changed on a regular basis; at the end of each academic year, we considered what 'tweaks' had to be made.

The key features of the practice in my PRU were as follows.

- All pupils were dual registered, which formalised our school partnerships.
- We developed an outstanding Tracking and Assessment proforma, which identified the pupils' needs and evidenced the progress they made.
- We held regular and planned reviews which brought the main players together.
- We created a Pupil Passport, which focused on what strategies we used and how this could be transferred to the mainstream school setting.
- All pupils attended their mainstream school, and this was gradually increased during their time at the provision so that the final reintegration was not seen as a hurdle.

- School attendance and increasing engagement in the pupils' learning was a priority.
- We supported the role of emotional well-being leads, which helped increase mainstream school expertise.

What should be included in the curriculum offer?

Some units believe they should internally provide the opportunity for pupils to follow the full curriculum, especially at Key Stage 4. This would mean employing a teacher with expertise in every curriculum area. This is neither financially viable nor practical. None of my pupils were penalised for not achieving eight or more GCSEs and prevented from following their post-16 options. I remember one pupil who was moving into post-16. He was asking if I would support his application and I said of course, as long as he didn't want to study Japanese! His face fell as that was a subject he wanted to study. Fortunately, the college gave him that opportunity despite not achieving a GCSE in a foreign language and he pursued this at university. I have never made that mistake again in not believing that a pupil can achieve their dreams!

The purpose of a PRU is to assess and provide interventions for the pupils' SEMH, which is the main reason for referral. Therefore, the curriculum offer should be a balance between academic subjects and a therapeutic curriculum which helps the young person to thrive.

Buildings and facilities

Unfortunately, most PRUs and APs are found in local authority buildings classed as 'waste' stock. These are generally buildings which are deemed to be not fit for purpose for the education of the mainstream school child or for adult workers. The facilities are limited, especially the access to specialist rooms or outside space. There is no clear directive on what classrooms should be made available in a PRU. There have been purpose-built PRU buildings and their design success has been down to a headteacher's vision rather than an architect's brief. Even then, they are often found in areas where transport is limited and they are on the fringes of main communities. I have seen PRU buildings which are placed on an industrial estate in an 'office'-based building but mainly in old school buildings which have significant health and safety issues. They are patched up to make them look better but the issues around leaking roofs and poor drainage are still there. I was once offered a building in the middle of an industrial estate next to a garage with no outside space and the pupils, if accepted, would have had to walk across this estate to the building. When I pointed out health and safety issues and of course safeguarding, they seemed surprised I was not grateful.

PRUs work with our most vulnerable pupils who have to leave their home communities to travel across towns and cities, usually independently, and be ready for school by 9am. I often find this amusing as the pupil who has had difficulty attending their home school, walking with their friends – their support group – is then expected to have the skills and incentive to travel an extra distance to a new school where they have no friends.

However, a fabulous building does not always mean the pupils are getting the best-quality teaching. That is, as I have shared above, down to the staff and what goes into the culture of the provision.

Schools' responsibility

Schools must arrange and fund AP for children suspended for a fixed period of longer than five days. Schools should ensure that pupils who are absent for a whole range of reasons are provided with education to complete at home or are referred via the local authority to support services. This may include:

- funding to support dual registration with the mainstream school;
- provision for all pupils who have been permanently excluded;
- pupils who are classed as non-attenders;
- pupils who are ill, whether this is short- or long-term illness;
- pupils with mental health issues;
- pregnant schoolgirls.

REFLECTIVE TASK

- What qualities do you look for when identifying a PRU or AP for one of your pupils?
- How do you quality assure this provision and ensure the pupils you place there are receiving high-quality education and support?

Local authority responsibility for pupils

For pupils who cannot maintain their mainstream school placement, local authorities have a duty to commission placements, not provide for pupils who may fit the list below. They also need to ensure that they have in place a quality assurance programme which can demonstrate these pupils are accessing a high-quality educational provision:

- time funding commissioning;
- permanently excluded pupils from the sixth day;
- non-attenders;
- pupils who are ill;

- pupils with mental health issues;
- pregnant schoolgirls;
- asylum seekers.

PRUs' and APs' responsibility

PRUs and APs are commissioned to provide for any of the above categories identified by the local authority and to work in partnership with their schools. No pupil should be left without an educational placement and potentially 'lost' in the system. To enable them to provide an effective provision they should be able to demonstrate:

- clear admission and exit criteria agreed from day one;
- assessment of need to support the EHCP process, if appropriate;
- a range of interventions which can be used by the mainstream school;
- joint relationships with mainstream schools for those not permanently excluded;
- a curriculum which helps pupils to re-engage with their learning and experience success;
- improved attendance and engagement for the pupils in education;
- training opportunities for the mainstream school and wider multi-disciplinary workforce.

Ofsted approach to PRUs and APs

PRUs and APs are subject to the same process and rigour from Ofsted as their mainstream school counterparts. While acknowledging that PRUs and APs are intended to be used as short-term interventions, Ofsted will gather and evaluate evidence under the following headings.

Leadership and management

- How well leaders identify, assess and meet the needs of pupils when they first begin to attend the PRU or other alternative provider, including pupils with SEND.
- How well leaders ensure that the curriculum is coherently sequenced and meets all pupils' needs, starting points and aspirations for the future, including through remote education.
- How successfully leaders involve parents, carers and, as necessary, other professionals or specialist services in deciding how best to support pupils.
- Whether leaders are ambitious for all pupils, and the extent to which those responsible for governance understand the particular context of the provision.

- How well leaders include pupils in all aspects of school life, giving particular emphasis to how well they are prepared for their next steps in education, employment and training, and their adult lives.

- How well leaders ensure that pupils' outcomes are improving as a result of any different or additional provision being made for them, including outcomes for pupils with SEND.

Behaviour and attitudes

In many ways this is the core purpose of the work of a PRU or AP. Pupils are placed there because their behaviour has been the main trigger for referral. So many pupils have joined my unit and there has been no evidence to suggest that there have been any significant safeguarding concerns but often within a few weeks these issues do materialise. This is not due to the school being negligent, but that the pupil began to feel more secure and have attachment to a positive adult.

In the same way as with other schools, inspectors will evaluate the ways in which leaders have made appropriate and effective safeguarding arrangements for pupils in the light of their higher vulnerability to safeguarding risks, including during the Covid-19 pandemic. Inspectors will expect providers to understand their unique contextual safeguarding factors and outline how they proactively work, including with other agencies, to mitigate the specific factors that affect their pupils and the community that they serve.

Quality of education

By default, most PRUs and APs have different objectives in their work, which should be related to the reasons why a pupil is placed there. The curriculum offer will be guided by the following.

- The needs of the pupil, the duration of placements and the proportion of time that pupils stay with the provider each week. For instance, in a PRU that provides short-term placements for excluded pupils or those at risk of exclusion, the core work may emphasise specific improvements in pupils' attitudes, behaviour and/or attendance alongside their academic/vocational/technical achievement or be aiming to reintegrate pupils into mainstream schools.

- APs may also offer services to schools and other educational settings to help them support children with additional needs in their settings.

- An AP setting may be the permanent destination for some pupils. Inspectors will evaluate schools' success in these areas, while bearing in mind that we expect high academic/vocational/technical aspirations for all pupils.

- When evaluating pupils' attainment and progress, inspectors will consider the ways in which leaders have identified, assessed and met the needs of pupils. They will evaluate the progress that pupils have made since they began to attend the AP.

Personal development

This is central to the work of a PRU or AP. Pupils don't feel good about themselves, and this is shown through the pupil either acting out or internalising their feelings. These provisions have the opportunity to develop the pupils' self-worth through a curriculum that supports the emotional and mental well-being of the pupils by developing their interests and talents to support progress and achievement. This can include the development of their physical and mental health.

Ofsted inspectors will also look at the following.

- *For pupils who have left the PRU or other alternative provider, inspectors will consider how well the progress they made there enabled them to move on to suitable destinations and, post-16, to take courses at an appropriately demanding level.*

- *They will also look closely at how effective liaison is with other schools to ensure that there are appropriately high expectations and, as far as reasonably possible, continuity in pupils' education programmes.*

- *Inspectors will also look at whether the provider works closely with families, schools and other agencies to ensure a smooth transition to and from alternative provision. They will look at whether it sets expectations that reintegration back into mainstream education is a key component of a placement.*

- *Inspectors will look at whether the provider has adapted the approach to securing a good transition for every pupil in the light of the COVID-19 pandemic.*

(Ofsted, 2023)

As with all schools, PRUs and APs need to be clear about the curriculum and what it is hoping to achieve. In some ways this is an advantage to the PRU community as they should be clear on the purpose and write it clearly under the following headings.

- **Intent:** what is the curriculum you are trying to construct and why? Will it meet the needs of your learners and enable them to make good progress?

- **Implementation:** do all your teachers have good knowledge of the subject(s) and courses they teach? What support will be provided to ensure that this is seen across the provision, including the use of resources?

- **Impact:** how do you know that your learners have made good progress and have developed skills and knowledge that will enable them to move either back into their mainstream school or into their next stage of education, employment or training?

Always remember that Ofsted is just one body that provides judgement on how good a job you can do. The real assessment is whether you can say you have done the best job for your pupils.

REFLECTIVE TASK

- Read the following quote. How would you respond to it, thinking about what you currently provide in your school?

For some young people education, including schooling, is a rich experience, a balanced mix of activities that stimulate and engage them, that prepare them for the future, and get them ready and able to face an adult world.

Yet for too many children, school simply becomes a holding pen until the age of 17, and until the age of 18 from 2015. If we continue to just keep children in education, without providing them with any tangible benefits, then we cannot bring about lasting change.

(Andrew Webb, cited in Cahill, 2014)

Final thought

When I first started teaching, I was fortunate to have a fantastic head of department. She taught me the dynamics of a classroom and how to perform. The most memorable thing she said to me when I started teaching was this:

Don't ever forget when you stand in front of a group of pupils you have to imagine you are an actress on the stage and you have to give the best performance you possibly can. Those pupils do not need to see your bad mood, your hangover or be the recipient of your bad temper. If you cannot do this then don't turn up. They deserve the best of you.

I have never forgotten this and have said it to my staff on a regular basis. While expecting them to give their best performance, you have to remember that sometimes a member of staff needs support and not to be judged; a good leader will always provide that.

KEY POINTS

- There is no 'I' in team.
- This is not rocket science – we all will experience SEMH issues in our lives, and we need the skills and understanding to recognise when we need additional help.
- If the provision is not good enough for your child, it should not exist.
- Provisions should have a clear remit of their purpose and work in partnership with their schools and local authorities.

- Investment in high-quality staff is essential to ensure that they can provide the best education for your pupils.
- Staff need to be creative and adaptable and not to be scared of change.

Further reading

Kulakiewicz, A, Long, R and Roberts, N (2021) *The Implementation of the Recommendations of the Timpson Review of School Exclusion*. London: House of Commons Library.

References

Baumeister, R (2005) *Rejected and Alone*. London: The British Psychological Society.

Cahill, J (2014) Achieving Outstanding in Alternative Provision: Speech given 23 October 2014 at Alternative Provision in Education Conference. [online] Available at: https://docplayer.net/46229359-Alternative-provision-in-education.html (accessed 28 February 2024).

Department for Education (2016a) *Alternative Provision: Statutory Guidance for Local Authorities*. [online] Available at: https://assets.publishing.service.gov.uk/media/5fcf72fad3bf7f5d0a67ace7/alternative_provision_statutory_guidance_accessible.pdf (accessed 9 January 2024).

Department for Education (2016b) *Educational Excellence Everywhere*. [online] Available at: https://assets.publishing.service.gov.uk/media/5a80b93d40f0b62302695246/Educational_excellence_everywhere__print_ready_.pdf (accessed 9 January 2024).

Department for Education (2019) *Timpson Review of School Exclusion*. [online] Available at: https://assets.publishing.service.gov.uk/government/uploads/system/uploads/attachment_data/file/807862/Timpson_review.pdf (accessed 9 January 2024).

Department for Education (DfE) (2023) *Special Educational Needs and Disabilities (SEND) and Alternative Provision (AP) Improvement Plan: Right Support, Right Place, Right Time*. [online] Available at: https://assets.publishing.service.gov.uk/government/uploads/system/uploads/attachment_data/file/1139561/SEND_and_alternative_provision_improvement_plan.pdf (accessed 9 January 2024).

Gov.uk (2022) Alternative Provision Census 2022: Business and Technical Specification Version 1.0. [online] Available at: https://assets.publishing.service.gov.uk/media/6095573fd3bf7f28907c2c62/2022_AP_Specification_Version_1.0_publishing.pdf (accessed 28 February 2024).

National Centre for Social Research (2022) Report: Children and Young People's Mental Heath in 2022. [online] Available at: https://natcen.ac.uk/publications/children-and-young-peoples-mental-health-2022 (accessed 28 February 2024).

Ofsted (2023) *School Inspection Handbook*. [online] Available at: www.gov.uk/government/publications/school-inspection-handbook-eif/school-inspection-handbook-for-september-2023 (accessed 9 January 2024).

2   What is SEMH?

Several years ago, I gave a presentation to a group of secondary headteachers about the numbers of exclusions they were issuing and the impact this was having on the PRU provisions. I had placed a bowl of pebbles in the middle of each of their tables and asked them to choose one. At the end I likened their pupils to pebbles on the beach, saying, *'There are many pebbles on the beach but each one is an individual'*. I asked them to look at that pebble the next time they were going to exclude a pupil and think about the pupil stood in front of them and the impact their actions would have on that pupil's future opportunities. A few days later a secondary head called me to share his story. He was about to exclude a pupil when he caught sight of the pebble he had taken and had placed on his desk. When the pupil came into his office, he said this pebble has saved you from an exclusion and that the woman who gave it to him would not be happy if he did indeed exclude him. That young man with support continued in the same school, completed his Year 11 and achieved quite a few GCSEs. This story is about second chances. Just after lockdown, I accidentally met this retired head in a garden centre. He brought up this story and said, *'I still have that bloody pebble!'*

Introduction

It's often quite easy to give a label for behaviours and, a bit like the word *'okay'*, a label actually tells you nothing about what it means or the way the person is feeling or how they are coping with a particular situation. I get so tired of listening to teachers who say that SEMH is not their problem but rather it belongs to colleagues in another part of the school for someone else to take responsibility for. All staff need to stop saying, *'Mental health is not really a teacher's job – our main job is results'*.

The aim of this chapter is to look at what the term SEMH means to you and for me to share what impact labels can have on the quality of education pupils may receive.

Labels, not a diagnosis

Since I started teaching in 1979, there have been a range of labels given to pupils who cannot for a range of reasons engage in their classroom and learn. I am a firm believer that this is not always the pupils' problem but is down to the way we teach and how we construct our lessons.

The labels I have worked with include:

- EBD: emotional and behavioural difficulties;
- BESD: behaviour, emotional and social difficulties;
- SEBD: social, emotional and behavioural difficulties;
- SEMH: social, emotional and mental health difficulties.

These are all in fact the same labels but as the years have progressed, the word '*behaviour*' has been removed and replaced with '*mental health*'. I once said that if we removed the word '*behaviour*', teachers would no longer have the excuse not to teach certain pupils and pupils would no longer have a reason to believe they could not be taught. It was hoped that by dropping the word it would encourage schools to see that behaviour is the way a pupil will communicate that something is not right. Schools need to stop focusing on the behaviour of a pupil and find out what is the underlying cause. Unfortunately, I now hear colleagues saying pupils have mental health difficulties which is why they cannot learn, so have we simply changed the word without trying to solve the problem? The inclusion of '*mental health*' within these labels, I had hoped, would encourage schools to look at what impacts on their pupils while they are in their school.

Some of the underlying causes of poor SEMH are:

- poor attachment history;
- bullying;
- trauma, for example domestic violence, abuse, crime;
- family dynamics.

But labels can be damaging. The words '*exclusion*' and '*suspension*' are negative words which imply that the actions of the person need to be punished, with that person removed from their current community. They are words more appropriately used within the penal system. While a label can damage a situation if incorrectly interpreted, by affecting a pupil's sense of self or conflicting with a parent's hopes and dreams for their child, labels can also be helpful to provide the right diagnosis. This can help direct a teacher to apply strategies and interventions which will be supportive to a pupil's learning and future aspirations.

Based on the pupils that came into my PRU and based on data collected over many years, I can say that in a typical class of 30 pupils, potentially:

- two will have experienced the death of a parent;
- eight will report having been bullied;

- five will have suffered from mental health problems;
- eight will have experienced severe physical violence, sexual abuse or neglect;
- three will be living in a step-family;
- ten of them will have witnessed their parents separate.

Many pupils may experience more than one of the problems listed above. From my experience, my pupils were more than likely to have experienced multiple problems once they had experienced one. Many pupils' issues arose from adverse childhood experiences (ACEs), which often derived from poor attachment and traumatic experiences.

One of the strengths of PRUs and APs is that they are very good at telling the story of the pupil, ensuring that this story can be shared accurately, warts and all! I will go into more detail in Chapter 3 about the work with our families but one of the things parents were fed up with was telling their story multiple times, so my role was to ensure that the story was told once, accurately.

REFLECTIVE TASK

- What does the label SEMH mean to you? Is it something your school has decided to allocate to a pupil through your own perception or do you collect information and carry out agreed diagnostic tests/assessments?
- Based on the life experiences shared by your pupils and families, would exclusion and suspension be appropriate for those with SEMH needs?

SEMH is a whole school issue

SEMH needs of pupils should not be delegated to a chosen, few members of staff, for example the school counsellor, pastoral leads or the special educational needs (SEN) team. All staff need to recognise that they have a role to play in ensuring that all pupils feel listened to and included. The response to SEMH difficulties involves an element of challenge and requires that a balance is found between:

- understanding 'the place' the pupils are coming from and their needs;
- protecting the rest of the school community from their ways of expressing themselves.

Pupils with SEMH need to be known and understood. In schools, SEMH can be seen in many ways, for example:

- mood disorders, which could be anxiety or depression;
- self-harming, which could be substance misuse, eating disorders or just feeling unwell with no medical explanation;

- problems with behaviour, defiance and aggression;

- a situation where SEMH needs are already diagnosed and the pupil may have a diagnosis of attention deficit hyperactivity disorder (ADHD)/attention deficit disorder (ADD), bipolar or attachment issues.

SEMH does not start in secondary schools at Year 7. Often the pupils have been contained within their primary school and these SEMH problems have not been fully addressed. When they transfer to the larger secondary school where they are expected to have developed independent coping skills, their SEMH comes to the fore and they are at risk of exclusion from day one.

For many of the pupils I have taught with SEMH needs there has been one major misconception, which was that these pupils by default must have learning difficulties. It is true that there may have been gaps in their learning due to a number of reasons, but many of my pupils did not have learning difficulties and did not require significant learning support. What my pupils needed was the opportunity to have some 'time out' so that they could rebalance their emotions and put into context the work they needed to complete and the coping skills they needed to achieve this. For many they did not need to be formally assessed and be given an EHCP, which for some could have been a barrier to their future aspirations.

I remember once going into my deputy head's classroom. One of the pupils who had been with us for about six weeks was completing some work independently. My deputy turned to me and said, '*Look, she is learning*', which I found a bit strange as this pupil had been settled for a few weeks. I looked at her, perplexed, and I looked again at the pupil, and I could see through her body language and her sense of self that indeed she was learning. She felt secure and supported; she knew she could ask for help and get it. That was something I looked for in all my future dealings and hopefully helped my staff to recognise in all our pupils.

Exclusion or suspension

For many schools, exclusion or suspension appears to be the only solution when the situation with some of their pupils' behaviour becomes unmanageable. But once an exclusion is placed on a pupil's record, it stays there and can have a detrimental effect on their future aspirations. Many pupils are excluded or are choosing to self-exclude because of:

- poor behaviour;

- undiagnosed/unsupported learning needs;

- mental health issues;

- the fear of failure.

What you need to be able to do as a PRU is understand the reasons why they are choosing to do this.

Being a pupil can be an uphill slog at the best of times, but being a pupil with substantial SEMH needs can be much tougher as they are often experiencing the following.

- Gaps in learning – this could be through poor attendance, ill health or simply being too anxious to concentrate in lessons and feeling they will never catch up.

- Disrupted exams and assessments – again, this could be ill health or a move into care where they have had to move to another area and school. The effects of Covid-19 are still affecting pupils' achievements.

- Getting on with teachers – as teachers we cannot like every pupil we meet; equally, not every pupil will like you. But you are the adult and need to find a common ground for working with that pupil.

- Keeping on top of schoolwork – never assume that your pupils have support at home and the necessary resources to complete homework. For some, they have little parental support; they could be young carers to their siblings or just do not have the energy to do any more work when they get home.

- Uncertain future – for some pupils it is very difficult to imagine their futures, especially if they feel they will never be good enough to achieve their dreams.

- Limited understanding by peers – for some, their peer group may be very challenging and they feel they just don't 'fit in'. Their peers may not be able to understand and provide the support they crave.

- Developing an individual identity – so many of our pupils struggle to understand who they are and where they fit into the jigsaw. If they do make choices, they are frightened of the response they will get from their family, friends and teachers.

If you can imagine learning to drive, which was possibly the last thing you learnt to do from scratch, try to recall how you felt. For most of us it was an unnerving and frightening experience. This can be compared to how pupils with SEMH feel every time they walk into a classroom.

REFLECTIVE TASK

This is an activity I have used in training to try and emphasise the above point. In a group ask four people to stand up and give them a balloon. Ask them to blow it up and tie it at the end. You need to then blindfold them and ask them to hold the balloon in front of themselves. At all times ask them how they are feeling. Walk around while you are talking to them so they can tell when you are close by. Begin to shake a box and ask them what they think you are shaking. Eventually someone may guess it's a box of drawing pins. Explain you are opening the box and removing a drawing pin, still walking around. Ask the people blindfolded if they are feeling more anxious and alert. Unbeknown to them you are also carrying a balloon and only the other participants in the room can see this. Stand behind one of the blindfolded people and pop the balloon. This often brings screams of nervousness and laughter. I did this exercise to align with how my pupils felt every day and every hour of their school day.

- How would you feel holding that balloon, and when you are anxious what skills can you draw on to allay those feelings?
- Ask the group if they could survive a day feeling that level of anxiety without displaying some characteristic of SEMH.

Warning signs of SEMH needs in pupils

There are key warning signs of SEMH needs in pupils, which can be identified as follows.

Observation

Have you noticed any of the following in a pupil you are concerned about?

- Decline in attendance.
- Rise in 'acting out' behaviours.
- Appears isolated and their friendship groups may suddenly change.
- Other pupils may express concern.
- Change in physical appearance.
- A known traumatic event such as a bereavement or a family breakup.

These signs do not automatically require an immediate response and I would suggest that staff apply a 'watchful waiting' technique, which is a technique that involves carefully monitoring areas of concern to see whether they get better or worse. I would recommend this as the majority of pupils who experience a 'dip' or a 'low' in their mental health can often get better within a few weeks without any interventions being applied. You need to be confident that, if used, a quick intervention or response will not exacerbate the problem.

Conversation and the art of listening

I'm sure everyone has heard the phrase '*I can hear you*', but are you really listening to what is being said? It is often the words not said and the body language of the person speaking which can tell you volumes about where they are emotionally at that particular moment. In the past few years due to Covid-19, most meetings now take place on Zoom or Microsoft Teams. I personally dislike these meetings as there is so much information lost in translation because you cannot read the room and the individuals' body language.

When people turn off their videos, how confident are you that they are indeed still in the room and listening? I find this can be so easily translated to how a pupil can feel when they are speaking to a member of staff; are they actually being listened to or are they already in another lesson dealing with another subject area? I can hear many teachers reading this and saying, 'But the pupils don't listen to me', and that may be true, but you need to ask why. Is your lesson interesting or, more importantly, can the pupil understand what you are asking them to do? Do the pupils feel you have 'already left the room'?

A pupil's SEMH is often brought to a head when something happens. This is the time when you need to listen rather than jump to a conclusion. When my pupils were angry, they would shout and charge around, upsetting everyone and everything in their path. I would ask the pupil to come and sit in my office, asking them to sit at the table while I finished the work I was doing. More often than not, I would pretend to be working but what I was doing was listening to their breathing. When you are in a state of high anxiety you breathe quickly. I would wait until their breathing became measured, counting up to eight between each inhalation and exhalation. By this point I would know if they had their emotions under better control. If they asked to speak before I could do this, I would say I was not quite ready to listen properly; I still needed some time to be calm and to give them my full attention. When I was confident they were calmer we would start the conversation, knowing that if they did get upset, they were in a position to self soothe and self-regulate their emotions. I would also at this point offer them a cup of tea: a simple act of kindness which most of my pupils appreciated. The following is how I would structure the conversation to get to the bottom of what had happened and why.

'What' stage – getting the facts

1. Give the pupil speaking your full attention – ask a simple question like 'What happened?' or 'What's been happening?'

2. Check you have heard everything they have said by repeating back what you have heard.

3. Clarify any points that you might not have understood.

'How' and 'why' stage – understanding their feelings

1. Ask the pupil how they felt and how it affected them. If the pupil appears upset or angry, say these words.

2. Create a link to a situation which you might have found yourself in and had similar feelings but don't make it about your experience.

3. Ask the pupil, 'How can we make this better?' Have they got a solution?

4. If they say this is hopeless or there is nothing I can do, challenge them in an unthreatening manner with possible solutions.

Assessment and tracking

It would be true to say that most schools function via the collection of data that demonstrates the academic performance and progress of their pupils. Aspirational targets set by the school usually have the goal of becoming one of the highest-performing schools in their local authority or across the country. The amount of academic assessment the pupils are put through is unbelievable and the tenacity of the collection of this information should be applauded. That is if you believe this is the only form of assessment which will demonstrate how good a job you are doing.

The assessment and tracking of a pupil's SEMH needs should have the same rigour, but again schools will often choose to restrict this data collection to the pupils they deem require it. It is not that difficult to establish an emotional tracking tool, which is something we did at my PRU as a collective. I therefore cannot take full ownership of the work we did, but it was shared with both primary and secondary schools and some chose to implement this across their key stages. It showed that often the pupils you assumed would need additional SEMH needs were functioning well, and this was especially true when we assessed Year 6 pupils on transition.

What should be seen in a SEMH assessment tool?

Like any assessment that you are doing, you need to know what you want to achieve and what outcome you are hoping to find. Following on from this, you need to ensure you will have the tools and resources to address your findings in the same way you would do using your academic data collection. Ask yourself:

- what is the purpose of this assessment?
- what am I going to do with it?
- how will I resource and fund this intervention?
- what is my intended outcome?

CASE STUDY

Interventions

In my PRU we developed a SEMH tracking tool, which was devised and refined over several years. We worked to implement a system that could guide any interventions we were to use for each individual pupil to enable them to return to their mainstream school better equipped and more resilient to face any further issues they might encounter. It is important to remember that we were not there to 'fix' the pupils but to help them gain the skills and strategies for them to negotiate relationships and environments which they found incredibly difficult on a daily basis.

Once we had completed the assessments, often in discussion with the pupil, we were able to identify their main barriers to learning. These could include difficulty forming meaningful relationships which resulted in them feeling lonely and ostracised in school, school anxiety, organisational skills, difficult home circumstances which impacted greatly on attendance and motivation, to name but a few.

→

As with any data, how that is used to then formulate change is the most important outcome. Over many years the staff at my PRU had developed a wealth of skills in working with SEMH, with individual staff concentrating on areas of personal interest to gain further training and qualifications. Each week we had a well-being session timetabled where every member of staff offered an intervention and the pupils, following the assessments and staff meeting discussion, were assigned to an eight-week intervention programme to address the issue we believed would help them to integrate back into school with the most success.

The interventions we offered were the following:

- dramatherapy;
- cognitive behaviour therapy (CBT);
- growth mindset;
- socialisation;
- team building;
- seasons for growth;
- therapeutic art;
- life skills;
- awareness of child sexual exploitation/grooming behaviours;
- forming positive friendships.

The impact of the intervention was also assessed and often helped to identify a further intervention should the pupil be staying for a longer package.

The belief in the PRU was that these sessions were as valuable or in many cases more valuable than the academic work as without honing these skills, the academic work would still remain a step too far for many pupils.

Data collection and tracking

When pupils were admitted to my PRU, we developed a clear tracking process which was contributed to by everyone who was part of that pupil's life. This is the process we followed.

1. **Information gathering** from colleagues from the mainstream school and the PRU staff and any other agency involved. We collated both the academic and emotional assessment and we carried out our own assessment within the first two weeks.

2. We then collected some appropriate **benchmarking data**.

3. In the initial six weeks we had **ongoing observations** while the pupil was at the PRU and when they attended their mainstream school.

4.   We put together an **initial draft plan** which included both the staff and pupils' views. I feel it is important that pupils need to understand what's been done to and for them and what's been done with and by them.

5.   At the first review, which was after four weeks, we had a planning meeting which added the **parents' and other agencies' views** to the plan.

6.   The **personalised learning plan** was agreed and this formed the basis of any future work. It was a working document and if things changed, then the targets were amended to reflect these changes.

What this did was ensure that any interventions or approaches we made were not based on anecdotal views but on the factual assessments which had taken place. This is really important, and I have made the mistake in the past of not fully understanding why we need to have this data.

Leadership in SEMH

The success of good SEMH in any school must come from the leaders within the school. You need to acknowledge the problem and how it can be solved, and liken it to doing a jigsaw; how do all the pieces fit together?

Figure 2.1 *Leadership responsibilities*

Schools could look at Figure 2.1 to begin to establish what they need to do to improve their approach to SEMH. This is not dissimilar to a chart you would develop to look at academic approaches and interventions.

- **Leadership in SEMH** – this means that all the senior leaders must provide 'visible' leadership in SEMH. Is there a named governor for SEMH who takes the lead and are they a member of the senior leadership team (SLT)?

- **Continuing professional development (CPD)** – what do you have in place on an annual basis and how is this CPD agreed? I would suggest that it should be based on the presenting SEMH issues within your school and what are the main triggers for poor behaviour. Does your school provide training throughout the year and revisit training sessions to ensure all staff are applying SEMH interventions?

- **SEMH strategy** – is there a clear and shared vision on what SEMH means within your school and how do you know this? The strategy should be linked to the school development plan and be seen as a force for change.

- **Data collection** – what does this look like and are all staff aware of how to identify and collate information on pupils who are displaying early signs of SEMH?

- **Staff accountability** – is there a culture of inclusivity and is there an ethos which fosters mutual respect and positive relationships between staff and pupils?

- **Reduction in suspensions and exclusions** – with an effective SEMH strategy, all pupils' needs will be supported and this should reduce both suspensions and exclusions within the school.

- **Attachment and trauma-informed staff** – as previously discussed, many of your pupils will have experienced numerous issues within their school life and pupils do not securely attach to their school community. This is more evident since the Covid-19 pandemic when pupils were isolated from their peers and teachers.

- **Prevention strategies** – what have you got in your bag to ensure that practical strategies can be applied in every classroom and by every teacher to demonstrate the corporate ownership of SEMH?

- **Specialist staff** – is there an identified emotional well-being lead and who else are the strategic leads across your school?

Adapting your classroom for SEMH

It would be fantastic if all pupils that walked into your classroom were academically and emotionally at the same starting point and ready to work. In reality, this does not happen and you have to ensure that your staff can meet the needs of all your pupils. Chapter 7 shares the World Health Organization's model of school-based mental health promotion which could be used as a model to develop your SEMH needs; it has a tiered approach for your interventions and who could provide them.

Throughout my years as a headteacher, I helped develop a range of resources which supported teachers in working with pupils with SEMH, but I would propose some simple things all staff can do to include all their pupils.

- Teachers should understand and be aware what effect their personal responses, both verbal and non-verbal, can have on a pupil's behaviour. My late husband said that I could destroy a person with one look. I was never aware of when I was doing this, but my pupils and staff would remind me that I had 'the look' and I had to apologise for the effect it had had on the group.

- Staff should be prepared for change as pupils with SEMH can change quickly and staff need to respond accordingly.

- Relationships are central to promoting good behaviour. Staff should be able to form positive appropriate professional relationships with their pupils.

- Teachers should understand why some pupils misbehave, why pupils can become more challenging and what action they need to take, which, if possible, is not always removing the pupil from the classroom.

Resources available which can be developed for SEMH in the classroom are vast and can be confusing. At my PRU we developed a range of resources which were used and shared with our partner schools and included in our initial teacher training (ITT) mental health course. There are examples of resources provided in the further reading/resource section.

Maslow's hierarchy of needs and SEMH

It is quite true that man lives by bread alone – when there is no bread. But what happens to man's desires when there is plenty of bread and when his belly is chronically filled?

At once other (and 'higher') needs emerge and these, rather than physiological hungers, dominate the organism. And when these in turn are satisfied, again new (and still 'higher') needs emerge and so on.

(Maslow, 1943, p 375)

When I was training to be a teacher many, many, years ago, I studied the theories of Piaget and Maslow to look at how as a teaching force we could impact on our pupils' lives. I was also interested in whether it could help to develop my own personal ethos of education and how this would affect my teaching in the classroom.

SEMH needs are part of everyone's continuum of need. Emotional well-being is an indicator of our social, emotional and physical wellness. It connects our mind and body, ensuring that as a whole person we can function and that our basic fundamental needs are met. You are also influenced by the relationships you have and the community in which you work and live.

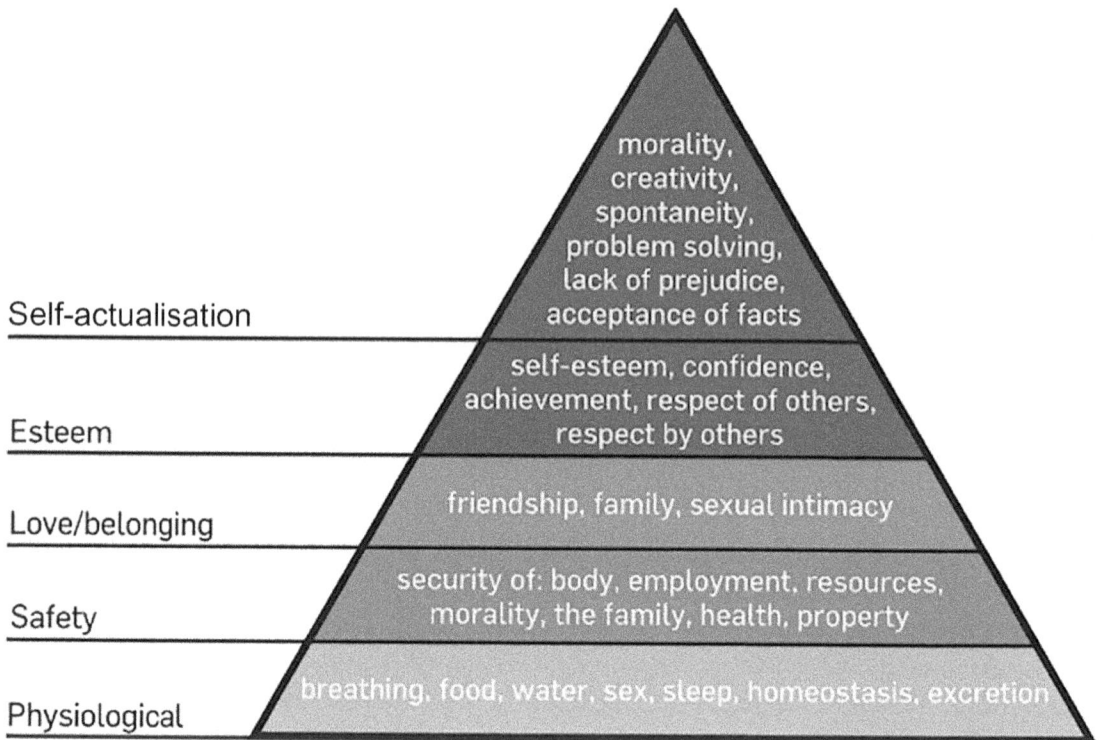

Figure 2.2 *Maslow's hierarchy of needs, adapted from Wikimedia Commons*

The key question when looking at Figure 2.2 is '*what does each pupil need in your school?*'

Maslow believed very few people are fully and continuously self-actualised. But characteristics of people with this state could include:

- reality is processed and interpreted fairly accurately;
- happy with their own identity;
- ability to tune and retune themselves into objective thinking;
- capable of appreciating day-to-day small experiences;
- multi-faceted and adaptable sense of humour;
- ability to establish deeper interpersonal relationships with a few people.

REFLECTIVE TASK

- What do you need to survive every day and to fulfil Maslow's hierarchy of needs?
- What do you need in your own personal arsenal?

I always carried my handbag and a bit like Mary Poppins I would amaze the pupils when I would take out all the things I needed to fulfil Maslow's hierarchy of needs. There was no wonder I had a stiff shoulder but every day, and before I do anything, I check that my handbag has the following.

1. **Biological and physiological needs** – a bottle of water and a biscuit.

2. **Safety needs** – I always check I have my car and house keys and that someone knows what I am doing and where I am going to be. I also have my mobile phone, which is fully charged, and if I'm going to London my son has the tracker on me!

3. **Social needs** – I know who I am: I'm a mother, a partner, a friend, and I carry a photo of my boys in my handbag and my work lanyard just in case I forget.

4. **Esteem needs** – I take pride in my work and I have staff who work with me and support me. I respect the work I do and I know my colleagues and friends respect me for the decisions I make. I also have my lipstick in my bag for support.

5. **Self-actualisation needs** – this is possibly the hardest part to achieve and can change on a daily basis. It is guided by the moods and experiences that each day brings. I often felt that a multi-headed screwdriver in my handbag would be very helpful so I could change quickly to respond to each situation I faced.

Behaviour policies in schools

So many policies in schools are punitive and unfortunately promote the denigration of pupils and how they feel. I know of schools where shouting at pupils is promoted – it can be a measure of how successful you have been in controlling the behaviour of your pupils. I rarely shouted because quite simply I could not see the point. Once I shouted, I had lost the argument because I was displaying that I could not control the pupil and their behaviour. My pupils could shout better than any of my staff and they could definitely play verbal table tennis with much more expertise. 'Verbal table tennis' was a term we used to describe a situation where you get into an escalating argument that neither participant is going to win. I once observed my deputy headteacher doing this with a colleague, and afterwards I asked what happened; basically, she had felt she was not being heard and that her point of view was not being listened to or taken seriously. This is how pupils also feel. My pupils were more concerned when I spoke very quietly; it appeared that this was the sign that I was becoming unhappy.

We all know that our behaviour is an expression of our emotions. I know that if I had not slept well or had a problem, my performance at work would be affected, but I still had to be able to deal with those pupils who were unable to leave their problems at the school gate. Sometimes when my pupils arrived at school, they were angry, often with the whole world, but basically they were sad or angry with themselves. They felt what they were going through was too hard, and in many ways this became an excuse for the way they were behaving. What I needed to do was to help them to accept that it is easier to blame everyone else for their failures rather than accept what they have contributed to their current situation and what they can do about it. You have to help your pupils find their own solutions to the problems they are experiencing and give them the tools to change what could be potentially sad outcomes. Pupils who have low self-esteem will self-sabotage any successes they may be having in their work or in relationships as a form of self-preservation. They behave in the way they do to protect themselves. One of my pupils would spend ages writing a piece of work, but if he read it and was unhappy, he would rip it up and destroy it. This meant we had to be very quick to remove the work and suggest we read it in the next lesson, which gave him time to reflect and read his work in a different mood.

PRUs and APs are well placed to help a pupil reflect on what has gone wrong and how they can move forward, showing that mistakes can be a positive experience, especially if they learn from what has happened and make changes to ensure that this mistake is not made again. You have to recognise that the pupil has the potential strength and ability to change.

> A school's approach to Mental Health and behaviour should be part of a consistent whole school approach to mental health and well-being. This should include providing a structured school environment with clear expectations of behaviour, well communicated social norms and routines, which are reinforced with highly consistent consequence systems.
>
> (DfE, 2018, pp 4–5)

The Department for Education document *Mental Health and Behaviour in Schools* (DfE, 2018) sets out each school's roles and responsibilities in relation to mental health and behaviour. This sits alongside the document *Behaviour and Discipline in Schools: Advice for Head Teachers and School Staff* (DfE, 2022), which offers guidance to school staff regarding the development of a school behaviour policy. Every school must publish their policy in writing to staff, pupils and parents each year. The school behaviour policy must aim to:

- promote good behaviour, self-discipline and respect;
- prevent bullying;
- ensure pupils complete assigned work;
- regulate the conduct of pupils.

I'm not sure I totally agree with the recommendations from these documents. I would question the contributors' practical understanding of working in schools with pupils with SEMH needs or if it is the case that their recommendations are based on their theoretical assumptions and perceptions. Are these documents inclusive and do they fully understand and include the spectrum of need seen in our schools, which tend to consist of a diverse and complicated community? The documents draw on the behaviourist approach of rewards and sanctions, which does not work for every pupil, especially those who have suffered a traumatic event and are deemed to have SEMH needs. Using this approach can retraumatise the pupil as it does not enable the pupil to express their emotions and learn to self-regulate. They are not written with an act of kindness but are punitive and demoralising.

CASE STUDY

T's story

T, eight years old, had become increasingly difficult to manage in a small main-stream primary school. A managed transfer to a local primary school had not been successful and was followed by a PRU referral. T had been described as a bully, and in a discussion at the point of referral a teacher had said to a PRU lead that the parents were '*nasty pieces of work*'. As T settled into the PRU, challenging behaviour and aggression was expressed towards their peers and teaching staff. One of the teaching staff commented how T seemed to have arrived fighting and that every-thing, every request, instruction or greeting, appeared like an attack that seemed to prompt a fight.

T's parents were separated; their father was from a travelling community and worked out of town at times and their mother had stopped working as it had been increas-ingly difficult to hold onto work when she had to respond to calls from schools to attend meetings or pick up T. As T spent more time in the school and the school spent more time with the parents, more of T's history became known. T's parents both had negative experiences of education; their dad had left school at around 13 years old, having been bullied most of his school life. T's mum had left school with no qualifications, having struggled with learning throughout her school. T was born 10 weeks premature and as a result had undergone several operations follow-ing birth because of a heart condition. T had been described since birth as a little fighter. The parents, who were in their early twenties when T was born, separated when T was around three years-old after T's dad was imprisoned following a fight in the local community.

T's case provides an example of how sometimes the dynamics that are being expe-rienced within a school can have a far-reaching legacy. The school's discovery that T had literally been fighting since their first days of life really helped staff start to think about T's needs differently. Previously, an assumption had been made, in part informed by early referral discussions and subsequently by the difficulties encoun-tered when trying to manage T's aggression in the school. Work with T's parents was undertaken in the main by the class teacher, who happened to spend many afternoons talking with T's mother as part of a daily debrief. To an outsider, some of these conversations may have seemed very trivial and unrelated to the school day. The class teacher was, however, very skilled and genuinely interested in under-standing T's circumstances and background and how T was relating to their mum between school days. In essence, the teacher discovered what life was like for them and how they managed. Due to these discussions, T's mum felt able to speak about her uncertainty about the school system and how she had felt let down by her schooling. She also talked about T's earliest months and discussed the great anxie-ties they had experienced as a family as T underwent different operations. T's mum

→

spoke about her insecurity of causing frustration and pain for T and avoided being authoritarian. This was the same for T's dad, who was also very sensitive to T's earliest experiences and consequently did not want to impose any further frustrations or pain. T's dad featured more in conversation and was invited to school. He started to attend meetings and debriefs as well and started to build up a sense of trust with T's class teacher.

The teacher's open curiosity and respectful enquiries allowed for the development of a working relationship that was free from brash moralising or hasty conclusions being formed. It was in this context that deeper understandings of T's needs and development were gleaned and the right support could be applied.

Emotional well-being lead

All schools have been encouraged to appoint an emotional well-being lead who can work alongside the SEND lead to meet the needs of those pupils with SEMH issues. I believe this role to be essential in all our schools when they need to have a better working understanding of their pupils' SEMH presentations. I would suggest the key purpose of this role would be to:

- deliver one-to-one support and bespoke sessions for vulnerable pupils focusing on engagement, attendance, achievement, well-being, personal development, social skills, welfare and employability;

- support the aims and values of the school as detailed in the school's statement of purpose, vision and values.

And that the key responsibilities would be:

- to provide individual support to pupils in need to enable them to re-engage and thrive in their school life;

- to provide ongoing mentoring and targeted sessions/programmes to support the SEMH needs of the pupils;

- to work alongside teachers to ensure that both academic and SEMH needs can be met in a unified way;

- to work closely with teachers and support staff to help plan effective strategies to support individual pupils;

- to fully understand individual barriers to learning with regard to learning, mental health, safeguarding and home circumstances and how these may impact on performance;

- to build a relationship with the pupil/parents/carers prior to coming to the school and helping, where necessary, with the induction process;

- to keep accurate records of interactions with pupils, parents/carers and other agencies.

REFLECTIVE TASK

I have always been in awe at the changes my pupils make during their time at my PRU. As I shared before, I always did the admission meetings and when the pupils arrived; they were often very angry and upset, some of them saying categorically that they were not coming to my rubbish school and that they could go back to mainstream and be okay. Although they recognised that they had problems and at times felt useless, returning to their mainstream or a new mainstream school felt like the better option. Coming to a PRU or AP was tough, as the pupils had nowhere else to go and had to accept that we were there to uncover all those feelings they had and to help them 'recover' so they could move forward. As I would say to them on many occasions, '*If you do not love yourself, who else will?*' Self-love is quite a big thing to acknowledge and we all have difficulties giving ourselves that.

I have read a book called *The Chimp Paradox* (2010), written by Professor Steve Peters. He asks three questions.

1.   Do you sabotage your own happiness and success?

2.   Are you struggling to make sense of yourself?

3.   Do your emotions sometimes dictate your life?

He explains the struggle that takes place within your mind and then shows you how to apply this understanding to every area of your life so you can:

- recognise how your mind is working;
- understand and manage your emotions and thoughts;
- manage yourself and become the person you would like to be.

The Chimp Model explains how the mind can be seen as three teams, each with their own agenda and way of working.

1.   The 'Human' you, mainly based in the frontal lobe, is associated with logical thinking and works with facts and truth.

2.   The 'Chimp', mainly based in the limbic system, is an independent emotional thinking machine and works with feelings and impressions.

3.   The 'Computer' is spread throughout the brain and is a storage area for programmed thoughts and behaviours. The Human and Chimp can both put information into the computer.

The key is to store helpful information in the computer to help manage your Chimp. The problem most of us have is that our Chimp often takes over our way of responding to situations and that can cause us lots of problems. Part of my work was to help my pupils

→

take control of their 'Chimp', and I have to say on occasions that was very challenging, but I hoped that my pupils understood much more about what triggered their anxiety and fears and what they had to do to deal with them more effectively.

With this information, ask yourself:

- Do you recognise your inner 'Chimp' and do you know what you have to do to control your Chimp and respond in an effective way?
- Do you self-sabotage the work you may be doing and can you reflect on the reasons why you do this?

Final thought

Positive SEMH impacts on academic progress and life chances. This is not a debatable statement but one you will recognise from your own experience and journey. When you feel happy, secure, supported and valued, your work output is more successful. Why then do schools not prioritise the development of these feelings in all their pupils? It has always felt to me that this was a win–win scenario – happy pupils, outstanding achievement – but schools need to find their own balance in how they implement this.

One of the difficulties I have had all my life is the inability to lie. What you see is what you get, and this was a characteristic my pupils valued as I never told them lies. They would know if I was trying to pull the wool over their eyes and pupils with SEMH needs who have received so much nonsense in the past will quickly work you out. The outcome of deception is that you lose their trust and respect, which has to be earnt: it does not come with your position. So be honest to your pupils and to yourselves.

I have given the following poem to every member of staff who has ever worked for me and to as many new ITT students that I have come into contact with. It has guided my professional career.

> I have come to a frightening conclusion.
>
> I am the decisive element in the classroom.
>
> It is my personal approach that creates the climate.
>
> It is my daily mood that makes the weather.
>
> As a teacher I possess the tremendous power to make a child's life miserable or joyous.
>
> I can be a tool of torture or an instrument of inspiration.
>
> I can humiliate or humour, hurt or heal.

In all situations it is my response that decides whether a crisis will be escalated or de-escalated.

And a child humanised or de-humanised.

(Ginott, 1972)

Please read and reread this poem and use the power you have to ensure every pupil, whatever their needs, has the opportunity to succeed in your school.

KEY POINTS

- There is no 'I' in team.
- This is not rocket science – schools and PRUs working in partnership should be the same as any other partnership developed by a mainstream school.
- You must remember that behind every graph and piece of data you have collected there is a pupil with their own story which is personal to them.
- To tell a pupil that they cannot return to the school they know is like telling them their life is over. Try to think of the long-term consequences of your actions.
- Keeping a child within the PRU/AP system long term does not solve the problem; it just contains or enables the problem to manifest itself.
- Remember how you respond to a pupil with SEMH may reflect your insecurity rather than theirs.

Further reading

Kerr, J (2013) *Legacy: What the All Blacks Can Teach Us About the Business of Life*. London: Constable.

Manson, M (2016) *The Subtle Art of Not Giving a F*ck: A Counterintuitive Approach to Living a Good Life*. New York: Harper.

Stockport Council (2018) *Improving Emotional Wellbeing: A Self Assessment for Education Settings in Stockport*. [online] Available at: https://democracy.stockport.gov.uk/mgConvert2PDF.aspx?ID=140262 (accessed 9 January 2024).

Whitaker, D (2021) *The Kindness Principle: Making Relational Behaviour Management Work in Schools*. Carmarthen: Independent Thinking Press.

References

Department for Education (DfE) (2018) *Mental Health and Behaviour in Schools*. [online] Available at: www.gov.uk/government/publications/mental-health-and-behaviour-in-schools–2 (accessed 9 January 2024).

Department for Education (2022) *Behaviour and Discipline in Schools: Advice for Headteachers and School Staff*. [online] Available at: https://assets.publishing.service.gov.uk/media/651d42d86a6955001278b2af/Behaviour_in_schools_guidance.pdf (accessed 9 January 2024).

Ginott, H (1972) *Teacher and Child: A Book for Parents and Teachers*. New York: Macmillan.

Maslow, A (1943) The Theory of Human Motivation. *Psychological Review*, 50(4): 370–96.

Peters, S (2012) *The Chimp Paradox: The Mind Management Programme for Confidence, Success and Happiness*. London: Vermillion.

3 Good communication and supporting parents and carers

My sons and I loved the film *Mrs Doubtfire* and we would watch and laugh at the escapades that Mrs Doubtfire would get up to. In the final scene, Mrs Doubtfire explains about all the different families that exist, and finishes with '*But if there is love, dear... those are the ties that bind, and you'll have a family in your heart forever*'. This sums up the many different families that exist and how they can be successful, whatever their dynamic. As a single mum not through choice but through bereavement with two sons aged six and nine years, I was both mum and dad. It was not easy but what often made it harder were the assumptions by other people, often professionals, who believed that being a single parent automatically meant that their children would be disaffected in school and this would be the main precursor to behavioural issues. How can anyone be so confident to label families and assume these things without much investigation? It was this rejection of labels that guided all my relationships with parents and carers and I tried really hard never to judge any parent that came through my door.

Introduction

It takes about seven seconds for our brains to compute and decide what kind of person we are meeting. Are they honest? Are they trustworthy? Do they know what they are talking about and understand what I am dealing with on a daily basis? If this is true, it is so important that in that very first meeting, you connect to the parents, carers and pupil seated opposite you or speaking to you on the phone. This is a make-or-break opportunity.

Unfortunately, PRUs' and APs' home-school relationships are seen by many parents and carers as the place where their child will have minimal educational success and their life journey is sealed to that of no or limited opportunity to do well in their working life. PRUs can often be seen as the place where pupils are permanently broken and will need support for the rest of their lives. Parents and carers can adopt the attitude that they just want their child to finish school so that all their problems will disappear and if they get some qualifications along the way, that will be a bonus. This attitude was often reinforced by mainstream colleagues who spoke about the move to a PRU/AP as the final punishment or destination. I have spoken previously about the perception many have of a PRU without ever having visited one, and until there is better partnership working between mainstream schools and PRUs this will continue.

For many of my pupils and parents, our PRUs were that conduit for change and the work we specifically did with parents not only ensured their child's successful return to school, but it often helped them to address their own negative educational experience and move forward. Parents would often feel ignored and pressured into sending their child to a PRU. This chapter looks at how parents can be more actively engaged in the process and what support can be made available through pupils' mainstream schools. It is also about parent empowerment, allowing them to take back responsibility for their child, and what the school and PRU can do to ensure positive parent/carer/child relationships are developed.

Emotional factors impacting home-school relationships

When a child is referred to a PRU or AP it is at a point in time when different pressures and anxieties are at their most acute. It is in the context of such pressure and anxiety that communications between home and school and vice versa can come under significant strain.

When schools consider referring a child to a PRU or AP, it indicates that something has gone wrong and is not working. There is a background to all referrals and, within all background circumstances, there is a history. This history and the role it will play is important and requires sensitive consideration. It is from within these backgrounds and histories that the scene is set for the underlying emotional dynamics that will influence the communications between home and school and vice versa. Supporting parents and carers as they enter and navigate the PRU or AP educational context requires a deep sensitivity and respect. The reason(s) a child might be referred to a PRU or AP can be varied. Paying attention to the emotional context of a referral is a very important feature of understanding how you might communicate with and in turn support parents and carers.

CASE STUDY

J was 13 years old when referred to a PRU because of concerns that 'mainstream' education was unable to meet their needs. Following transition to secondary school it had become increasingly apparent that J's ability to manage the demands

---

of a larger environment and a more varied timetable brought with it challenges that were overwhelming them. J seemed to have become increasingly anxious and withdrawn; they were less communicative, more rigid and obsessional in how they got ready for the school day and didn't seem to have any friends. J stopped wanting to attend school and their attendance became problematic. J's parents were surprised by the change in J's personality. They described how J had always been quiet but was generally cheerful, happy in their own company and had interests they liked to focus on. J had generally seemed well and progressed throughout primary school.

In one of the first meetings with the secondary school to discuss J's faltering attendance, a member of staff had referred to J as possibly being autistic. This comment had deeply upset both parents. They didn't really know what autism was and couldn't believe that J was being described in this way. After the meeting they searched the internet to find out more about autism. They couldn't believe that they might have missed something or not understood something about their child and as a result felt guilty. J's parents were now hopeful that the specialist PRU would be able to make further assessments and that J may have the opportunity to learn and make friends in a small educational setting.

J's parents were very anxious about how their child was progressing and felt a mixture of guilt, shame and embarrassment following the school meeting. The member of staff did not mean any insensitivity in their reference to autism, yet a dynamic was set up in which education professionals seemingly knew more about J than J's parents did, which resulted in the upset. This could have undermined future working relations with school staff, but the parents were able to work with the PRU to support future assessments. This was mainly due to the work of a key worker who worked closely with J's parents as further assessments were undertaken. The key worker did not know the family or J and worked in an open and enquiring manner. Their interest in J's development harnessed and mirrored the parents' endeavours to understand how J was managing and relating to their experiences. These close relationships between J's parents and key worker were very important for both the family and school as both parties were wanting to get to know J better. It was this relationship and of course the wider activities of the school and child development professionals in which further assessments and understanding took place. Further understandings and learning about J took place over time at a pace that was in step for both J's parents and the school. This avoided further sweeping 'diagnosis' or labelling of J's needs. J's assessment at the PRU took place over two school terms; following this assessment a further two terms were spent at the PRU before a successful transition back to a mainstream setting.

The parent and carer experience

Some parents have a real barrier towards engaging with school, either due to their own experience of lots of terrible 'parent' meetings or because they had a bad time when they were at school. Many parents have experienced or are experiencing mental health issues or trauma themselves and they are anxious before they walk through your door, with their emotions on high alert. Before that first meeting you should show you are credible, that you want to help and support them. Schools can be scary places for them so options on how to eliminate some of these anxieties could be offered, such as:

• offering to meet somewhere neutral which can remove the school-based environment and help break down that barrier;

• making the visit at home so you can see their environment, not to judge, but so you can begin to put into context some of the issues they may have.

Setting the ground rules

I always felt it was really important to set the ground rules with parents and carers from the first meeting. It was important to get to know each other and to ensure that this went as well as it could. To do this I would establish the following.

• Find out their name! This seems so simple but often assumptions are made about how a parent needs to be addressed and whether there are two parents or a single parent. Asking their name makes them realise you are asking about them and making the effort to know about how they parent and what support they have. I remember receiving a phone call from my son's school from his head of year. He asked to speak to one of his parents. I explained I was the only parent and if he had looked at his file, he would have known this. I know he went on to make the same mistake a week later. He missed the seven-second rule on both occasions!

• Call them by their surname – first names can be over familiar and unbalance the teacher–parent relationship.

• I always did the admission meetings as it was important for me to meet the family and for them to meet me – they could apply the seven-second rule and know who

I was, that I was accessible and that I wanted to get to know them. My title was headteacher, but I was still an educationalist trying to help their child.

- Let them know your name and how they should address you – I was never Janice to any parent or pupil. I know in many PRUs and APs that parents and pupils do call the staff by their first names. There is no published research that I am aware of that says this improves the relationship and behaviour of pupils in PRUs and APs. I applied this rule simply because when a pupil returned to their mainstream school, all staff were addressed by their surnames. Why create another hurdle they had to cross on their reintegration when they may unwittingly use the member of staff's first name?

- Establish an open-door policy – parents and carers could contact me at any time and if I was not available, I would ensure I would ring them by the end of the day with the agreement that I could call them up to 7pm, which was my cut-off point. If I was not available my deputy would contact them. I had one mum who would ring me every morning at about 9.30am. This was not to discuss anything of importance but just to talk. I would have to say to her very firmly that I had to go and would tell her I would be putting the phone down, which I did. This might sound rude, but she would ring me the next day and say, '*I bet you get sick of listening to me*' and laugh. I was just someone on the end of the phone to listen to her. What we did do was help her access a women's group where she could go and make new friends.

- Be clear what your role is – the first place is to support a parent/carer's child and to help them return to school but never to take full or joint parental responsibility. They knew there was no hidden agenda. What I said I'd do, I did.

- All my pupils were dual registered and I made it clear that their child was still a member of their home school and that this three-way partnership of PRU, mainstream school and parent/carer would be developed and strengthened.

- At the admission meeting, the exit plan was always established with a caveat that it may change as we completed our assessments.

- Be honest, but kind.

Rules of engagement

How you deal with parents and carers can significantly impact on the success of your pupil both academically and emotionally. While the above sets the ground rules, you need to ensure that you have a clear role of who you are in this partnership model. Here are a few of my tips.

- Do what you say you are going to do. There's nothing more frustrating for a parent to sit in a meeting being promised actions that never materialise.

- Never ever say, '*I know how you're feeling*'.

- Try to break down the barriers they may be feeling about the school – their own school experience will possibly be guiding what they say and do. You have to try to break this cycle of negativity so they can have a positive experience of teachers.

- Be consistent in everything you do.

- Challenge parents but always with support and try not to be judgemental. If you are asking them to do something, put in the stepping stones to help them be successful. During one of my Ofsted inspections, the inspector came out and said the parents were scared of me. I felt really upset about the language he used but he corrected himself, saying that the parents said that if '*Mrs Cahill asked you to do something you had to do it*'. On further investigation what he did find out was that we worked well together – we all contributed to the outcome and we all had a role to play.

- Remember you are not the parent – you will not be taking on that role and they are not your friends – don't become so familiar that your professional relationship becomes blurred.

- Signpost parents to agencies who can get more fully involved and provide specific support. This will ensure you can do your role of engaging the family in the educational journey.

- Tell the child that if I had supported their parent/carer to do something and they were cross about that request, then they needed to come in and talk to me the following day.

Parents and carers are your service users. They can contribute to the success of your school and it is important that they are treated as a valued customer. They should be given a good experience when coming to your school so that they will come back and work with you. Hopefully, the next time you phone them to talk about their child, you will receive genuine support and a willingness from them to talk to their child about what went wrong. They will share the responsibility to improve their child's behaviour and attendance.

REFLECTIVE TASK

One of the issues I was faced with was a complaint from a parent regarding the communication they had with a staff member from the pupil's mainstream school over the phone. They had felt talked down to and criticised. They said it always made them feel they were being told off and they needed to singly do something about their child's behaviour in school. The staff phoning rarely explained what the school were going to do and when they did mention the school's plan of action, this was often punitive, saying that if their child's behaviour did not improve they would have to look for another school or face possible exclusion.

- What do you do in your school to ensure that every parent receives a quality-first experience when being told about an incident which has impacted on the other pupils from your school?

- What training do you put in place for your staff who are expected to make that phone call home and how do you quality assure that there is an expected standard for all staff?

- What does your school ethos say about how you work with parents and carers?

Safeguarding

It always amazed me that when a pupil was referred to the centre, there were rarely any safeguarding concerns given, but within a few weeks the pupil had shared with us incidents and experiences that sat within safeguarding guidelines. This is not a criticism of the school, but because the centre provided a safe environment and I had shown that I did what I said I would do, the pupil knew that action would have to be taken and that they would be supported in that disclosure. On admission I would tell parents/carers and pupils about the following.

- My staff and I would not keep secrets and if pupils began to make a disclosure, they would be stopped and it would be explained that this information would be shared with the designated safeguarding lead (DSL) and possibly social care.

- I would be clear about what I would do if there were safeguarding concerns and explain that safeguarding processes were non-negotiable, and sometimes they may be unhappy with that call from social care and not myself.

- Full safeguarding information was never shared with all the staff and they were told only what they needed so that they were safe when teaching and working with that pupil. For example, we had strict guidance around lone working and PRU to school transport, especially if the pupil had a history of making allegations against staff.

- Home visits were logged. Staff would call before they entered the pupil's house and they would have to ring within 20 minutes to say they were leaving the house. If we had not heard within 30 minutes we would call them. This was to ensure they had left the house safely. Once a colleague made a home visit at the end of the day and when she went into the home, the parent pushed her through a door which she assumed was the door to the living room. The mum said the dog had soiled in the kitchen and she needed to clear it up first. In fact, the door was to the cupboard under the stairs and there was no handle on the inside and she could not get out. Her mobile phone had no signal. She had left her place of work, was due to have a meeting with me and then had to collect her child from nursery. All she could think was that she would not be registered as missing until the nursery was closing and that I would assume she had another meeting to go to. After 45 minutes, she eventually got out of the cupboard and arrived to see me. It was an awful experience. You can never imagine something like this happening, hence the strict guidance we implemented above and through our lone working policy.

- I would explain that when I had to make a safeguarding referral, I would not accept any abuse or threatening behaviour from them.

- I would carry out the Family Team Around the Child (TAC) approach and not just standard TACs as the chances were the whole family was in crisis, with other children being affected by their sibling's behaviour. This proved to be very successful; in the first one I arranged, the primary school headteacher attended and she questioned her invite as the sibling did not seem to be showing any major concerns. Following the meeting she acknowledged the importance of understanding the whole family dynamics and the pressure they were under. Collectively, four children were given additional support by their schools and a range of other agencies, which prevented social care being involved and ensured the recording was kept at school level.

CASE STUDY

Many of the parents I worked with were very young and struggled with the teenage behaviours of their child sometimes due to the age difference that existed. I had one pupil aged 14 whose own mother was 28. Her mum had a new relationship and children with her new partner and worked so hard to be in her words a *'good mum'*. Her daughter disclosed she had been abused by a family member and I reported the disclosure officially. On investigation, there was no evidence to support the allegation, but the child continued to make allegations and comments about her family and she was placed in foster care for a period of assessment.

On this occasion, I had to help this young parent to adopt a stronger parenting style. She had no parents she could rely upon and in these exceptional circumstances, I had to be more of a kinship parent to the family but the ground rules were still clear. I was not the parent.

Support for staff

All staff will experience a safeguarding incident within their career. These can be very distressing and you must ensure that all staff have accessed basic training and understand the school's safeguarding procedures on an annual basis. They should know never to keep secrets and should be confident that they can tell you what they have seen, heard and done. This could be significant as the DSL has all the safeguarding information, and whatever has been shared could be relevant and be a sign that things are not going well.

In my centre we had a debrief every night. This was to share how the day had gone and was very supportive for all staff, especially if they had had a tough day and were feeling drained. This meant that the staff could 'pass their monkey' and go home with a clear conscience, knowing they had passed the problem upwards. If needed I would arrange a private debrief for that member of staff and ensure they had someone they could talk to. Occasionally, this would demand that a professional counsellor was available to listen to what they had heard and provide support. Cakes and biscuits also played a very important part of this debrief and especially when the centre was going through a particularly tough phase.

REFLECTIVE TASK

I have been involved in many safeguarding cases which have proved difficult; I always had to remember that I was not the parent but rather someone who would contribute to the multi-agency meetings about the next steps. I was also in the fortunate position to investigate and listen to the stories the family had to tell and how their journey to the point of needing safeguarding interventions had unfolded.

- Thinking about your school, what are the main safeguarding concerns that arise?
- Are you confident that your safeguarding is consistent across your school and how often do you quality assure?
- What are your current procedures for staff and could these be improved?

Key worker

Most parents feel isolated as their own experience of parenting a child showing anxiety and SEMH issues does not appear to be the 'norm'. Even if they have parental peers, they may not be experiencing the same 'trauma', leaving them to feel they have no one to talk to. When their child was referred to our centre, I would allocate them a key worker, someone who they could open up to and share in confidence what they are going through. In the early years of my headship, I often held this role and I felt privileged that the parents would trust me. The initial meeting was either in the home or at a neutral venue, for example a café where they could talk in confidence without interruption.

What can the key worker achieve or do?

The role of a key worker, who can be a teacher or teaching assistant, should never be underestimated. They are in the fortunate position to talk to the parent or carer in a more informal way. They can ensure that the footwork is done and provide additional support. Some aspects of their role could be:

- to help facilitate a change in parenting style;
- to provide practical support, not just emotional, helping the parents/carers to form interests outside the home;

- to set up meetings that can help them access additional support, for example information on youth groups and women's/men's groups which can support their mental health;

- to set up group parenting where the key worker can take parents for a walk in a local park and have a coffee. Many of our parents had never had this opportunity to put their own emotional needs first;

- to arrange school-based parenting support groups where you can arrange for other professionals to come and talk about problems – for example, a mental health worker, drug and alcohol worker, a social worker or an emotional well-being lead – so that their roles can be explained. This would again help to reduce barriers and any stigma parents and carers may associate with these roles;

- to empower the parents to take back their parental role. Often the children who walked through my door were the parent due to the emotional turmoil and crisis the adult was going through. Either I or the key worker needed to help re-establish the child and parent relationship, to reset the balance of power and to show who was the adult. Many parents needed to learn that they were a parent, not their child's friend. It sometimes felt they needed the permission of their child to parent.

One caveat that I always provided was that staff could refuse to work with a child and parent if they felt it was going to be too difficult for them due to their own personal experiences. Sometimes it is not in the best interest of anyone to ask a member of staff to support a family when they have experienced a similar difficulty. Not only can it bring up bad memories but their support, advice and guidance may be impacted by their own experience.

Supporting parents and carers: what should this look like?

I have always maintained that in the first few weeks I worked harder with the parents than with their child. Why? Because I needed them to support the work my staff were doing with their child. We needed to trust each other and understand what plans we were putting in place and that they were achievable. I would never be so arrogant as to feel I knew that child better than the parent and carer did; I needed them as much as they needed me to carry out my work.

When working with parents and carers I used the three counselling core conditions as my framework.

1. **Unconditional positive regard** – most parents have often only heard the negatives about their child but my role was to highlight the positives, showing the parent that I could see the good in their child. Often in a system where they may be struggling, it was so important to show parents their child is more than a number and more than their struggles.

2. **Empathy** – for the parent and carer, acknowledging that what they are going through is a lot too. Demonstrate you are trying hard to support their child.

3. **Congruence** – once I had built good building blocks, I could pick my moments to be more straight-talking but only once I had established that trust. Sometimes I had to give them some home truths about their child or their parenting but that could only come from a place of mutual respect first.

Breaking down the barriers with teachers

Parents and carers often have a negative view of teachers. This could be of your own making because sometimes you only contact the parents when things are going wrong. One of the things I did every week was make a phone call home. This was to share what had happened, the good and the bad bits. When I made that first phone call after admission to the centre, the immediate response from the parent or carer was *'What has he/ she/they done now?!'* When I began to share the good things, they often found this overwhelming and I often had tears at the end of the phone.

Many parents and carers had adopted negative views of their children because of their behaviours and would struggle to say or do anything positive about them. Many parents never saw their child as being any good and would often blame them for everything that was going wrong in their family, including personal relationships. This was a difficult issue to navigate and often the parent felt they had to make a choice. Was it the child's needs or their partner's needs which took priority? Unfortunately, it was sometimes the child that was sidelined, and my job was to highlight the needs of their child and that these should take precedence over their own. Often it was necessary to reset the imbalance between the child and adult, prioritising the needs of the child over those of the adult and not the other way round.

I also had to accept that sometimes I was not going to win with the parents or carers as sometimes they did not want to work with me and they were unwilling to put the needs of their child first. This was distressing but, in those instances, it was even more important that I kept on doing my job because I was not only the main support for that child but also modelling what a good relationship could look like so they could eventually, and hopefully, form healthy relationships elsewhere. I had one pupil whose parents were just completely uninterested in her mental health difficulties and gave her a really hard time; she sat with me every morning crying about situations from the night before. The problems the pupil shared were never serious enough to call social services about but my role was about being a constant person for that pupil.

So, what are the benefits of investing time with parents and carers? I found that the impact of good support can influence many areas of a child's life. Teachers, parents, carers and the pupils themselves can recognise the benefit of receiving good support, which can have an impact on all parts of their lives.

I found that with good support:

- classroom learning improved and the burden on the teachers' classroom management and teaching reduced;

- parents and carers said that their relationship with the school had improved, as had their relationship with their child;

- according to pupils, their home life improved after support and their approach to learning was much better. They were themselves seeing progress and were proud of the work they were doing. They once again had an aspiration to achieve.

Parenting styles and who is a parent

I don't feel that labels and categorising things into groups is helpful. It can unwittingly create a barrier and a stigma to the type of parenting that is being offered but I think it is important to recognise that there are groups that need a special mention in this chapter. As shared earlier, there are clear ways of working with all parents and carers no matter who they are but for some I would need to ensure that my way of working was more specific to their needs and circumstances.

Looked after children

There is clear statutory guidance for looked after children (LAC). There can be and should not be local interpretation of how these vulnerable groups of pupils are supported. LAC are generally:

- children who may be still at home but are LAC;

- children removed from their families and living within a foster care placement;

- children who have been placed in a children's home, which may be within their home local authority or on occasions many miles away;

- children who are placed in a hospital setting or a secure setting for their own safety.

For many LAC placed outside their local area, going straight into a mainstream school is not viable, as it is potentially not safe for the child and unfair for the receiving school who may not have the information to provide the necessary support. These children often feel they have failed – their families, their peers and mostly themselves. They feel they are to blame for whatever reason they find themselves in care. I needed to be confident that these children could experience success and feel a sense of achievement. If that meant being in the centre for a short period of time for assessment to take place then this in the long term could reap substantial benefits. They needed a time for adjustment, and this gave the centre the opportunity to get to know the pupil. By the centre carrying out an assessment of both their educational and SEMH needs, when the pupil moved to their named mainstream school the school was then confident they could meet the pupil's needs, making the transition and inclusion to the pupil's new school successful.

You should never decry the experiences these children may have had; as adults, it can make difficult reading when their files are shared. They are generally highly traumatised through their life experiences and removal from their home community. They are often very angry and will go out of their way to sabotage the relationship you are trying to establish. I needed to ensure that within the educational system, we were not creating more problems and that the transition to school was as seamless as it possibly could be. Building relationships with the care home staff was on occasions challenging due to various working patterns of staff and there could be several lead workers. I had to ensure there was consistency in the advice and expectations I had from the care home and the home authority.

CASE STUDY

One of my pupils was referred in Year 10. She had spent several months in a psychiatric unit and then within a secure residential home. She had been placed in care due to significant family abuse. She had cut her hair off and tried to burn herself on many occasions. When she started at the centre, she wanted to establish who was in charge and she believed it was her. However, she did also develop significant positive relationships with the staff, especially my deputy at the time. Within the secure base we provided and that provided by the care home, she flourished, became less angry and engaged with her education. In one of her English lessons, she was asked to write something about her future and how she felt about it and these were her words:

> This is life, a wonderful gift. Accept it, embrace it. It starts with a new day, wake up and greet it.

I had this put on a big banner and it sat on our hall wall for all our pupils and staff to read every day. I believe it had impact on all our feelings every day but also made sure that mistakes made yesterday were not carried through to the following day. We all started with a clean sheet of paper.

Adoptive parents

Children who have been adopted are often aware of the family makeup very early in their lives and know that the parents they live with are not their birth parents. For many of these children there are few problems, but like all children there a few who will struggle and while their attachment to their parents has been strong, this can be weakened in their teenage years.

Kinship care parenting

I had not really identified my 'different parents' with this label but this kinship care parental responsibility demands better recognition by the professionals involved. Many of the pupils I worked with were not officially LAC but lived with either a family member or family friend through agreement with the birth parents. Social care rarely became involved in these arrangements unless the child had been at risk of becoming LAC and this placement was by far the better outcome. I was always in awe of these very 'different parents'.

There was often little choice in their decision to take on this child, as they felt an obligation to look after their family member. For whatever reason they had in agreeing to take on parental responsibility for a child, for those who could be displaying SEMH needs there were extra considerations. But I saw how well this worked for so many of my children. The kinship parents I worked with included the following.

- Grandparents. The role of a grandparent is very special. They have been a parent and the relationship with their grandchildren is generally not being the disciplinarian but the one to provide softer support. However, taking on this role means they have to revert to the parent and this can be very difficult. They have to re-establish boundaries while still acknowledging that the parent is still there, possibly living in the same home or close by. The dynamics of everyone's relationship has changed.

- Aunts and uncles when the parents' circumstances have changed. This often involves bringing the child into their own family unit with cousins who they may or may not get on with and applying the same rules, even though they may want to provide a softer touch due to the child's experience. To the existing family, they must show 'fairness'.

- Sisters and brothers, who again may have their own children but will bring another child in.

- Family friends who have no biological attachment.

Formally, kinship care can include:

- children who may be 'looked after' by the local authority and are placed with kinship foster carers;

- children living with any of the above through an informal arrangement with the parents;

- a child that is placed on a child arrangements order or special guardianship order.

CASE STUDY

I had one pupil whose mother died, her father was not around, her younger brother was placed with a family member and other family members were unwilling to take the girl on as she was in Year 10 and quite challenging. She was at risk of permanent exclusion for poor behaviour. We were asked to support her just after her mum died. Fortunately, her mum's best friend had offered her a home; this proved to be a really positive outcome as the family friend never gave up and encouraged the girl to continue with her studies: she went on to enrol on a college course and gain her own independence. Can you imagine losing your mum, your natural home environment and your school within three months? I think many adults would struggle with all those changes but despite her young age, and with the support of this kinship care parent, she did well.

Restoring the relationship balance with restorative practice

Restorative practice, or restorative justice, has been used under many guises throughout my educational experience. Whatever name this technique is given, the main and most important factor is that it aims to repair damage done and restore relationships.

There are five long-standing principles of restorative justice/restorative practice.

1. Relationship.

2. Respect.

3. Responsibility.

4. Repair.

5. Reintegration.

I found that this was a very powerful tool when relationships between parents, carers and pupils had been severed, which often contributed greatly to the child's struggles at school and building trusting relationships with other staff and pupils. All the staff I worked with were trained in this approach and each had the main questions on cards in their lanyards to remind them of the language they should use with the pupils. These were:

- what happened?
- what were you thinking when it happened?
- what did you feel inside when it happened?
- how are you now?
- who else has been affected?
- what do you think you need to feel better?
- what needs to happen to make things right?

Children and adults need to be able to mend relationships that have been damaged. They need the opportunity to:

- tell their side of the story;
- express their feelings;
- understand better how the situation happened;
- understand better how it can be avoided next time;
- feel understood by the others involved;
- acknowledge the harm caused;
- find a way to move forward;
- feel better about themselves.

Restorative practice was often used when the relationship between the mainstream school and the parent, carer and child had broken down. I would use the review meetings as an opportunity to reset the relationship with the school and especially the teacher who had been the main contact with the parent. The parent would blame the teacher for everything that had gone wrong, which was generally very unfair. They had been the one to tell the parent about the behaviour and the school's response was not their personal response. To ensure that the pupil could return to the school successfully, this relationship needed to be restored and past misunderstandings settled.

CASE STUDY

One pupil I worked with presented as almost mute when she arrived and only spoke to a select few members of the staff when she started to settle. She was living with older foster carers who had an old school approach with her and had expressed that they often struggled to understand her moods and behaviours. On one occasion, her foster mum arrived with her and asked to speak to the teacher. The foster mum had put money into a birthday card she had given the pupil but had found this money in the bin. The teacher asked if the foster mum had discussed this with the pupil, but she hadn't. A restorative meeting was suggested to help her to understand what was going on and the pupil readily agreed to this with the support of the teacher. What transpired in the meeting was that the pupil was not ungrateful for the gift but was very upset that her birth parents had not done this for her.

After this meeting, the relationship between foster carer and pupil visibly improved and the lines of communication were opened!

REFLECTIVE TASK

- How do you ensure that problems are solved in your school?
- Do you use restorative practice/justice to help mend the problems that occur between pupils and between pupils and staff, and how effective do you find this approach?

Attachment

There are numerous books on attachment, for example, *Attachment and Emotional Development in the Classroom: Theory and Practice* (Colley and Cooper, 2017), and I would direct you to read the many outstanding academic books on this subject. However, I did see every day poor attachment demonstrated by my pupils. They were often 'lost' and felt poorly equipped to be positive about their home and school relationships. In a PRU it is much easier to foster good attachment, especially if the staff are effective communicators and can demonstrate what good attachment can look like. Through all the work

I have discussed above, I did help pupils to securely reattach, not only to their school but more importantly to their parents, carers and family in general.

When working with pupils I would observe insecure attachment through the following behaviours.

- Pupils appearing to be independent, self-contained and self-sufficient.
- They had learnt that showing vulnerability is unsafe, not to show feelings and emotions, and that the quickest way to obtain approval is compliance.
- Pupils would blame themselves for their problems.
- They would withdraw but could also get involved in cruelty and bullying towards others to 'feel safe in the crowd'.
- They would attempt to obtain parents', carers' and teachers' responses by increasing their emotional behaviour – in terms of being happy, sad, angry and demanding.
- Pupils would destroy work they had completed in class, especially if you had praised it.

I will discuss attachment in more detail in Chapter 4, as attachment to your school can be the main link to pupils achieving and making good progress.

Final thought

All your staff have to be able to demonstrate an open and respectful curiosity, time and a neutral attitude when working with parents, carers and pupils. You must remember that when a referral to a PRU or AP has been made, something has gone wrong. When things are going wrong, pressures and anxieties are at their height. Pressure and anxiety can impede and undermine communication and can undo even the best intentions.

> *There are only two lasting bequests we can hope to give our children. One of these is roots; the other, wings.*
>
> (Hodding Carter II, 1953, p 337)

KEY POINTS

- There is no 'I' in team.
- This is not rocket science – relationships with parents and carers need the same consideration that you would give to any other professional relationship you are nurturing.
- Establish the working relationship from day one.
- Never believe that you could be a better parent to their child.
- Do not allow their excuses for poor parenting to become yours.
- Keep the parents and carers accountable just like they will keep you accountable if action is not taken.

Further reading

Department for Education (DfE) and Department of Health (DoH) (2015) *Promoting the Health and Well-Being of Looked After Children*. London: DfE and DoH.

Gerhardt, S (2007) *Why Love Matters*. Hove: Routledge.

The Kinship Care Charity (2023) [online] Available at: www.kinship.org.uk (accessed 9 January 2024).

References

Colley, D and Cooper, P (2017) *Attachment and Emotional Development in the Classroom: Theory and Practice*. London: Jessica Kingsley.

Hodding Carter, W (1953) *Where Main Street Meets the River*. New York: Rinehart and Company.

Mrs Doubtfire (1993) Directed by Chris Colombus [Film]. 20th Century Fox.

4 Inclusion

The term 'inclusion' can be both challenging and divisive. I have attended and contributed to so many conferences on inclusion, and in the end it boils down to providing an educational provision that meets the needs of your pupils. I shared my opinion and perception at one of those conferences, at which I coined the phrase '*this is not "rocket science"*', where I showed a group of pupils sitting together, enjoying each other's company alongside a space rocket leaving Earth. Schools have all the equipment to create an inclusive environment. They just need to stop making it so technical.

Inclusion is different for everyone. You can talk about feeling included within your family or friends. At times in your life, you may feel excluded by the actions of others, resulting in you developing coping skills to accept this and move forwards. Within the school environment, there is an assumption that pupils will feel included just by attending but if you do not provide an inclusive school setting, pupils may become so disadvantaged that they are excluded in all their future aspirations. Inclusion is not a tick box or a certificate on the wall of your school. Inclusion is a living, breathing activity that is visible and felt by everyone who contributes to the school community.

Many years ago, I moved my PRU from a derelict school building to another old school whose physical building was in a better state of repair. When one of my retired colleagues came to help clean the building, she said, '*The feeling has come with you*'. It felt the same. That made me think that inclusion is an emotional as well as a physical action, and it should be felt wherever you are. I was determined that every pupil that walked through the door of my PRU would feel included.

The following poem was written by one of my ex-pupils. He had been removed from school following an incident outside of the school day. He had taken some drugs and had been missing from home overnight. His friends had left him and he came to my PRU as he felt he could not cope with the big mainstream school setting. He needed some 'space'.

Happiness

Happiness is rich, silver and gold.

It is a sparkler, not knowing when it's to burn out.

It feels like being wrapped up in silk hoping it won't untangle.

It tastes like an everlasting sweet.

Happiness sounds like a tropical island.

This was pinned on the board in front of my desk for 24 years. It made me remember why I did the job I did. He wrote this when he said he felt attached and safe. I hope this chapter can provide my interpretation of inclusion.

Introduction

There are many definitions and interpretations of the word 'inclusion' and if I asked you to provide your definition and share this with colleagues, the chances are you would all see inclusion as something different.

The government's definition of inclusion appears to change on a regular basis so it would be unhelpful for me to quote what they believe. But I would suggest that schools need to respond to three questions so that they can look at and review their current inclusive practices and the impact these might have on vulnerable pupils at risk of exclusion.

1. How can PRUs/APs and schools work better together to promote an inclusive local culture?

2. What does best practice on inclusion look like and what else do schools need to do to better deliver this?

3. What action is needed by local authorities and government to improve inclusion across the local and national education system?

These are two definitions that I like within the myriad that can be found on any search engine.

> *Inclusive practice refers to a teaching style that acknowledges and makes space for the different ways in which children learn, and accepts that different children will benefit from different learning techniques depending on their needs.*
>
> (Twinkl, nd)

> *Inclusive education means all children in the same classrooms, in the same schools. It means real learning opportunities for groups who have traditionally been excluded – not only children with disabilities, but speakers of minority languages too.*
>
> (Unicef, nd)

The main problem that schools and PRUs/APs face when talking about their inclusive practices is figuring out what inclusivity means. But I believe what this highlights is the need for schools to create their own definition which should be dependent upon the school's ethos and community. The school's definition or vision of inclusion needs to be exclusive to the school itself, without excluding those pupils with identified additional needs including SEMH and how you can best support these pupils. Inclusion is personal and schools have to ultimately decide what it looks like to them. In my centre, inclusion was defined as the five PCs.

1. Positive contribution.
2. Positive communication.
3. Positive creativity.
4. Positive co-operation.
5. Positive confidence.

My staff and I believed this embraced inclusion and how we could do it, and we personalised our offer to include the words above. Words without meaning or substance have no impact at all.

What do statistics tell us?

As previously mentioned, data and statistics can provide support in understanding why pupils are excluded and what happens to them. According to analysis by the County Councils Network (CCN), as of 2023, the number of pupils with an EHCP is 517,026 and rising on a daily basis. It is suggested that 180 pupils are given an EHCP every day (Weale, 2023). Schools are expected to fund the first £6000 of support with local authorities picking up the remining costs. If we turned our thought process around and said, '*What can I do with £6000 for a pupil before they are allocated an EHCP?*' can you imagine the impact this would have, not only on the school's budgets, but on the emotional development and academic achievements of these pupils? Should you be asking the question: while the allocation of an EHCP is important, are the ones being given really needed? Would it not be better to invest in the school's system so pupils' needs can be better identified and supported at an earlier stage?

Other figures of concern are that in 2022, more than a million days of learning were lost due to suspensions, with the number of girls being suspended rising by 59 per cent. In 2023, 58 per cent of the prison population had been excluded from their allocated school.

The PRU/AP population is made up of a greater number of pupils than just those who are permanently excluded. There are 16,732 pupils who attend PRUs, AP academies or free schools and other provision like FE colleges. This doesn't include a further 9897 pupils who also attend AP but have a mainstream school as the main school at which they are registered. According to the House of Commons Education Committee (2018), 22,848 pupils are also educated in other forms of AP, which include, but are not exclusive to, independent schools and providers that are not able to register as a school. These statistics are a damning inditement of our education system that is not meeting needs; we cannot continue to 'pass our monkey' or pass on the problem.

If these statistics are correct, does this help promote inclusion or create further division over what a school should provide? Do you need to take a different approach? I have read a book called *Our Iceberg is Melting* (Kotter, 2006), which is about a penguin colony whose home is in danger. The fable is about the initial resistance to change, but with information and clear leadership, obstacles can be overcome. Sometimes we just have to think outside of the box.

Containment in any part of the education system for someone else to sort out when that pupil moves key stages or schools is not good enough. SEMH does not develop when a pupil enters their secondary school. The problems they have had have manifested over many years, and due to the structure of the primary school many problems can go unnoticed or the problem is contained. I remember one pupil who had been allowed to play in the primary headteacher's office for the final term of his primary school and had then transitioned to his secondary with minimal information of his problems being shared. Within four weeks, this pupil could not be supported safely within the school for both his emotional and physical well-being. My PRU became involved to support, but with joint planning in the summer term before transition, my involvement would not have been needed.

What does inclusion mean to a child?

I don't know any teacher who would wake up and think, '*Who can I upset today and make them feel unhappy?*' As shared in a previous chapter, we cannot like all our pupils all of the time but there are staff who have set out to deliberately target pupils they don't like and who they feel they need to 'get one over' on, making their lives hell. I watched *Shirley Valentine* (1989) a few weeks ago, and there is one scene where the headteacher asks what was man's most important invention. Shirley knew the answer but the headteacher asked several other pupils who either were deemed to be her favourite or had in her opinion more intelligence. When they each got the answer wrong, she told Shirley to give her answer as she said you might as well get it wrong too. Shirley actually answered correctly, '*The wheel Miss, it's the wheel*', to which the headteacher accused her of cheating, and that in effect was the end of her school career. In one single action her enthusiasm for learning and good behaviour went out of the window. Have you ever seen this happen in your school?

Why might teachers do this to pupils? Possibly because those pupils are a bit different and do not conform to what they believe is a 'good' pupil, and those pupils make them feel anxious. I have always said that you can only feel love and hate because it is based on your own experiences and feelings. If you hate something it is possibly connected to things you have done or experienced, so to hate or dislike something in another person, you have to understand that emotion.

We think that by treating others the way we would want to be treated we are fulfilling their needs. I would regularly say, '*Treat others the way you would want to be treated because at the end of the day you have to look in the mirror and see your own reflection and accept the things you have done, both good and bad, during that day*'. However, should the better approach be to treat others as they would want to be treated? To do this requires the teacher to understand and have knowledge of pupils' needs and how to support them. In an article (Goddard, 2019), Professor Willem Frankenhuis suggested that instead of asking what is wrong with these pupils, we need to ask what is right for them. By understanding pupils' needs better, we can design interventions that harness and develop young people's talents. Rather than trying to reshape pupils to fit the school context, we need to look at how we can change the context to fit the strengths of the pupils.

This is not asking schools to change to fit the needs of each individual pupil, which would be unrealistic, but it is asking schools to understand their cohort: what makes their school different to the one across the town or city and what are the main needs of their pupils?

I was lucky enough to work with some headteachers who chose to be inclusive at the cost of Ofsted and league tables; they believed in the needs of the pupils and that their staff would give the pupils a 'second chance'. They chose not to be selective like some of the heads who would look at a pupil's academic profile first to see if that pupil's overall GCSE grades would enhance their own end-of-year results. I think I would call this unconscious bias/selection. Another practice I observed was schools offering Year 11 places at the end of January, meaning the results achieved (which could be negative) would not be added to their current Year 11 results. How can you call this inclusion?

REFLECTIVE TASK

- How do you ensure that your staff are meeting the needs of the pupils in your school and are demonstrating inclusive practices?
- Have you asked the pupils what they believe would be their ideal teacher?
- What do you think their responses would be?

When I asked my pupils this question, they explained what they wanted from a teacher, but it boiled down to a simple request: relationships.

Looking at the following list, what training do you provide to your staff to enable them to feel confident in their classroom practice and develop positive relationships with their pupils?

My perfect teacher:

- understands it is hard to be a teenager;
- doesn't label me;
- is calm and does not shout;
- is chilled out;
- is patient;
- sees my strengths which might be hidden
- listens and sees me as an individual;
- can spot problems; and
- wants to build a relationship that works for me.

How do you demonstrate inclusion?

It is easy to say '*This is an inclusive school*' and to write reams of rhetoric and show data of why you can make this statement. But, like lots of things, there are times when you do not always want to celebrate. At these times, you may often be less enthusiastic to share what you have got wrong, feeling that any suspension or exclusion must mean there is a deficit in your practice.

The cohort of pupils I supported are young people that schools have worked with but who have not succeeded within the demands of that environment. Part of my job was to breathe new life into them. The exclusion of pupils and their families from the school community, who should have been the first to provide them with the attachment they craved to give them a sense of belonging, has far-reaching consequences. All children in educational settings should be able to access support to help them to overcome obstacles and trauma and build resilience. A whole school approach to supporting the development of good mental health is identified by the Department for Education as a positive factor for child and adolescent mental health. A robust approach to well-being should be supported through both the curriculum and safeguarding practices.

Maintaining the placement of a pupil with SEMH issues is not always attractive and the question you need to ask is: What attracts a school to keep or take on pupils with SEMH issues? Ofsted and school league tables are detrimental to a lot of schools doing what they know to be right, but I would ask why does Ofsted not ask about how many school uniforms you have provided and how many free school meals you have given to those pupils who do not meet the criteria to receive them? Do these questions say more about inclusion within your school than what your academic results show? The way schools are judged to be successful is often seen in one word and it is often this word that deters schools from supporting pupils with SEMH issues. To put it simply:

- if every pupil has not achieved eight GCSEs then they have *failed*;
- a grade from the exam board says pass or *fail*;
- a word from Ofsted says pass or *fail!*

Or using my English teacher's analogy of Ofsted, '*You used to be able to win a football match by scoring goals; now you have to be able to score goals while being able to do ballet!*'

But inclusion should be the thread that runs through every school and its community.

How do we build inclusion?

Most pupils will turn up and attend wherever they feel they are going to be motivated and that it will be beneficial to them in the long run. Learning should be enjoyable – that's not asking teachers to put on a fancy-dress costume and perform tricks; rather, when schools reflect on their inclusion practice, they could identify the potential barriers for pupils turning up and being successful. Many of my pupils would share how they felt when they turned up at school. Many felt different and were shamed by teachers when they could not answer the questions asked or had not completed their homework. It could be that they were choosing not to follow instructions but underneath that could be masking another issue they felt they could not share with their teachers. I remember a Year 11 pupil being referred in the November of her final year. She appeared to be depressed and staff shared that she was a lovely girl who was for some reason not coping. As with all our pupils, we carried out a range of academic and emotional assessments so that we knew her baseline and staff could address her needs. We found out that she had a reading age of seven and could not complete the coursework and the individual work she was now expected to do. She had relied on her school friends, who had always been prepared to help and support her. Her learning needs had gone through primary and secondary school unaddressed.

I believe that schools should investigate the potential barriers to their pupils' learning by considering the following aspects.

- Emotional learning barriers – do pupils feel supported? How do your staff address pupils' failures? Is this in a supportive way or in a punitive way?

- Motivational learning barriers – do your pupils see the bigger picture and benefits of attending school? If these barriers are not broken down into small steps, pupils will continue to feel they will never achieve and give up.

- Personal learning barriers – how do your pupils perceive their own ability and the opportunity to succeed? Do they believe in their abilities and what they are told by their teachers? When I was at school, my maths teacher told me every lesson I was useless because I could not grasp basic mathematical principles. Maths became my fear and therefore I believed I would never be able to do it. This feeling lasted and impacted me into my adult life. I did overcome this eventually, thanks to the fantastic maths teachers and pupils who never gave up on me.

Incentives for dual registration and inclusive practices

Schools and educational establishments can make significant contributions to the lived experiences of children and young people, and should be part of a multi-agency approach to build resilience among children, young people and families in the community. Often, schools and colleges choose to enhance the offer of support to their pupils by engaging the services of outside agencies. Most commonly this includes the use of counsellors, but is this enough? Should schools be engaging a range of therapists that can provide interventions that are not based on 'talk therapy'? It is important that schools and settings take reasonable and measured steps when engaging such services to ensure they meet the highest safeguarding and appropriate recruitment standards.

Many schools will identify an alternative pathway for those pupils who they know are struggling, especially as they move into Key Stage 4. There are some fantastic examples of how schools use both registered and unregistered provisions in the AP sector. They carry out their own risk assessment so that the pupil will be safe and supported, ensuring also that attendance at the mainstream school continues so that the pupil can still access English and maths education and potentially achieve external accreditation. The problem arises when these provisions are used and the pupil has no contact with their mainstream school and there is an assumption that all their needs are being met.

CASE STUDY

I was asked to set up a provision initially for pupils who were LAC and were in out-of-area secure provisions due to their mental health needs. It was felt that these pupils were removed from their home community and when they returned, often post-16, they had little if no support. The provision we established was supported by the Child and Adolescent Mental Health Service (CAMHS) and social care, and collectively we made a difference. As the provision developed, the pupils referred were usually still within their mainstream school and few were LAC as the need to move them out of area decreased. We became a joint school/PRU/CAMHS provision, which removed many barriers.

We developed a thematic curriculum where the pupils were taught all the individual school subjects but through a different medium which enabled the pupils to learn without the negative association of a maths or English lesson. The pupils did not initially attend their mainstream school until they had spent at least one term in the provision, by which time we had built up their confidence and self-esteem and the transition back to school was highly regulated. For most pupils, their initial reintegration into the larger learning environment involved moving into the main PRU as reintegration here began as soon as the pupil started. I will discuss reintegration fully in Chapter 6.

The ethos underpinning the curriculum at that provision was one that sought to provide a consistent, stable and flexible approach to pupils' education. The objectives of the curriculum offered were the following.

- Six themes were carefully selected to be taught as discrete packages over the academic year, approximately one theme every half term.
- Pupils received a personalised and differentiated learning package to enable Key Stage 3 and Key Stage 4 pupils to access the appropriate age-relevant curriculum.
- Each theme encompassed the core curriculum subjects and incorporated other foundation subjects.
- The overall yearly programme provided an appropriate curriculum balance given that individual themes were weighted towards certain subject areas.
- In addition, the curriculum included activities which enabled pupils to develop social and practical skills in the wider community.
- Creative opportunities for recognised accreditation were accessed to reflect the pupils' learning needs.
- Academic, emotional and social assessments supported teaching and learning.

- The curriculum enabled pupils to make a smooth transition to their mainstream/special school, the main PRU or their post-16 destination.

All the programmes of study shared a common format.

- An importance statement described the important aspects of the subject, explaining what pupils could expect to gain from studying it, and identified how it linked to the aims of the curriculum.
- Key concepts identified the main ideas that pupils needed to understand in order to deepen and broaden their knowledge, skills and understanding.
- Key processes identified the essential skills and processes that pupils needed to learn to make progress in the subject.
- Range and content outlined the breadth of subject matter from which staff should draw when teaching the key concepts and processes.
- Curriculum opportunities identified opportunities to enhance the pupils' engagement with the subject through visits to museums and activities in the community.

By making these connections between subjects, events and activities, staff were able to design coherent learning experiences that were meaningful and relevant to the pupils. Staff were able to use more innovative teaching styles, choosing how learning was organised, where it took place and who should lead it. Pupils experienced a curriculum that was more relevant, provided the support and challenge they needed and better met their interests and aspirations. At all times, consideration of the pupils' mental health status was paramount.

> *The curriculum should be treasured. There should be real pride in our curriculum: the learning that the nation has decided to set before its young. Teachers, parents, employers, the media and the public should all see the curriculum as something to embrace, support and celebrate. Most of all, young people should relish the opportunity for discovery and achievement that the curriculum offers.*
>
> (Mick Waters, Director of Curriculum, QCA)

There were many learning opportunities between my PRU and mainstream school and we were often the conduit to other statutory services, for example CAMHS.

There has been a move in recent years for schools to either set up an internal alternative pathway or create their own PRU on site. This way, they continue to have overarching control of what their pupils are receiving and also ensure that the move back into the mainstream can be quicker and more effective. In reference to my earlier comment, schools know their pupils and their needs. If there are not enough PRU places then, with financial acumen and foresight, these facilities can be set up internally and be successful. Schools have a real opportunity to learn from each other as they develop their own internal provisions.

Inclusion of pupils with long-term medical needs

One group of pupils which are often overlooked are those pupils with medical needs. Schools can become anxious about having a pupil in school who may have a myriad of health issues and the school will use their health and safety policy to justify their reasons for saying the pupil cannot be in school. However, I have witnessed the effective use of technology to ensure that pupils who need to be educated off-site for a short period of time can continue to learn and have access to their peers and teachers. Many home tuition services will provide education in the home and this is generally time limited. Within my home tuition service, my tutors would have contact with the mainstream school and deliver the syllabus on behalf of the school so that when the pupil returned there would not be any significant gaps. This was especially important at Key Stage 4, and I would allocate specialist English, maths and science tutors so that their knowledge of the subject ensured high-quality teaching. The work completed was marked by the tutor and also the mainstream teacher to ensure that the marking process reflected the standard of the school. It also helped when the pupil could see comments from their teacher and I would encourage mainstream staff to contact the pupil, if possible, to 'check in' and help remove any potential barriers to reintegration.

CASE STUDY

Using technology to include pupils with medical needs – AV1

Pupils with medical needs are often overlooked when it comes to inclusion as their attendance is sporadic because school has to fit around hospital admissions and appointments, alongside periods where they are adversely impacted by their illness and cannot attend school. Technology can be used to support these pupils in feeling included, maintain their peer networks and continue to feel that they 'belong' to their school community, despite their absence.

AV1 is a telepresence robot that has been trialled extensively in schools to support pupils with medical needs. The small robot becomes the eyes, ears and voice of the absent child, and its physical presence reminds teachers and peers that it represents a real child. The child can see all that is happening in the class via an end-to-end encrypted live video stream that is not recorded. Their voice comes through a two-way speaker in the body of the robot with a volume control for modulating the output for different class tasks. Operated via a tablet wherever the unwell child is located, for example from a hospital bed, they can indicate how they are feeling through facial expressions as well as through speaking. The head flashes when the child wants to ask a question or remains blue when the child is too unwell to participate and just wants to listen.

Teachers have reported that using AV1 is better than teaching remotely or setting work as they have no additional tasks other than ensuring that any worksheets or books are either delivered to the house or emailed across. Peers report that they have enjoyed the opportunity to remain in touch with the absent pupil and support them while they are away. Schools have used AV1 in creative ways to make the pupil feel truly included, such as making the robot part of a drama scene, taking the robot on school trips and enabling it to go out at break times.

Pupils with medical needs have found AV1 transformational. They have felt that they have remained connected with their home school and their friends and know exactly what is going on as they are virtually attending their classes. Anxieties about returning to school when they are well enough are also minimised as they are up to date with their work: this means that reintegration following absence is seamless, therefore minimising the risk to them falling further behind as a consequence of their illness.

AV1 is still being used across the country by hospital schools, mainstream and special schools and PRUs. It was funded using DfE Innovation funding, initially in Northamptonshire where it is still being used with great success. As we move forward, we must embrace technological solutions for inclusion for this cohort of pupils.

When pupils are admitted as inpatients to regional psychiatric provisions, they move not only from their school but also from their families and immediate community. I was appointed as the executive head of a regional psychiatric provision for a short period of time. Pupils who were admitted were provided education within the on-site school. Prior to my appointment, the attendance of the pupils was not consistent and when the pupil left the provision support to reintegrate back into their mainstream school, their report was not supportive and did not provide guidance on what their learning needs were. I will talk more about this work in Chapter 6.

Supporting the inclusion process through partnerships

I am a firm believer that mainstream schools and PRUs/APs have to work collectively and not only within their own footprint. Pupils do not technically belong to a school but to the wider community, which is generally overseen by a local authority. If pupils are moved, then they must still be educated and schools need to work in partnership with other institutions to see how this can successfully happen.

Schools need to have a good understanding of the PRU/AP that they may use for their pupils. One document I would recommend is the Alternative Provision Quality Toolkit, which was published in 2022. The document sets out a framework for all providers and referrers to the AP and outlines a checklist of essential criteria of what a good AP should provide.

There are 13 quality areas which sit under three categories.

1. **Community** recognises that AP schools and providers are part of the wider educational eco-system that safeguards and supports pupils. Strong relationships and effective partnerships are crucial components of AP quality.

2. **Curriculum** accounts for the support and education provided to pupils. It draws attention to aspects that are particularly pertinent for AP settings such as pupil induction and quality of education, as well as physical and mental health and well-being.

3. **Currency** focuses on the outcomes and value gained by pupils in AP, including personal development, academic performance and successful transition to appropriate destinations.

The toolkit enables schools to take a balanced approach to evaluating the effectiveness of an AP and provides an extra tier of assessment for schools in determining and supporting their decision to refer a pupil to the PRU/AP.

CASE STUDY

Several years ago, the exclusions in my authority were very high. I was asked to set up a provision and reduce exclusions by 50 per cent, which was quite a tall order. However, with the support of my team we developed a provision called Prevent, Provide, Return (PPR). In partnership with eight mainstream schools, we provided each school two places a week for 12 weeks on a part-time basis. The scheme was established for two years so each school would send 12 pupils and we would support a total of 96 pupils over the two years. The aim of the project was to reduce exclusions, both fixed and permanent, within the partner schools through the offer of an alternative strategy for those whose behaviour for learning was starting to cause concern despite the usual tiers of in-school support. The most important factor was that schools shared the funding of this provision. They invested in their pupils before they reached permanent exclusion: they thought outside of the box.

The aim of PPR was to work with mainstream schools to provide a programme of support to enable each pupil to develop confidence, self-esteem, a sense of responsibility and behaviour for learning so that they would become successful learners within their mainstream school.

The PPR provision accommodated up to eight Key Stage 3 pupils on a part-time basis for three days each week. This model enabled 16 pupils to access the project each term, for example, eight in the first half of the week and eight in the second half for a maximum of one term, Wednesday being an overlap day for both groups; therefore, across three terms, this would create 48 places each year. With eight participating schools, each school had the opportunity to refer six pupils in any academic year. Schools who found they did not need to use a place in a given term entered into an agreement with another school in the partnership who could take up the place. In reality, this never happened.

Referrals needed to be in accordance with the agreed PPR protocols as the success of the project required that the appropriate pupils were referred to the project. The referral criteria were designed to ensure that a referral could not be considered for those who had needs so complex that a specialist placement was a more appropriate pathway. School leaders referring to the PPR needed to feel that a creative part-time placement of this kind was likely to address the pupils' needs and enable them to return to their mainstream school without requiring long-term support. All partners had agreed to responsibilities under the PPR agreement to maximise the likely impact of the project for the pupil. The PPR project partnership worked together to:

- ensure that all relevant assessments, both academic and in relation to SEMH, were carried out;
- support families and carers, both in support for their children and when in crisis;
- link with all external agencies;
- ensure that effective safeguarding was in place.

Communication between the staff and the school was essential and schools would send a member of staff to the PPR project on a Wednesday to support the day and be the link for that pupil when they were in school. Written reports were emailed at the end of the weekly placement to the mainstream school, with the mainstream school also sending a report so that we were prepared for any issue that had happened at either site. On the two days the pupils were not attending PPR, they attended their mainstream schools and accessed lessons as normal. This was to ensure their links with the school were not broken. It also provided an opportunity for them to take newly acquired understanding and skills quickly back into the mainstream environment.

It was also important to work closely with our parents and carers as they often had negative relationships with their child's mainstream school and we had to help 'build bridges'. Parents could contact the centre lead and there were regular review meetings to ensure that progress was being made.

The PPR programme served as an opportunity to identify and unpick the difficulties a pupil may be facing in school. This was carried out through specialist assessments and day-to-day observation by experienced staff. These assessments informed much of the work carried out with each pupil. Parents, carers and a mainstream school representative were invited to attend a halfway review after six weeks to discuss the assessments that had taken place and the progress made. A final meeting took place at the end of the programme to enable everyone to celebrate progress

→

made and to share classroom strategies and further intervention programmes that would benefit the pupil.

The pupils followed a thematic curriculum and had sessions on:

- re-engagement with English;
- re-engagement with mathematics;
- study skills;
- social emotional aspects of learning;
- restorative approaches;
- outdoor education;
- team building;
- therapeutic art and drama.

And to ensure that there was a comprehensive understanding of the pupils' needs, the team carried out the following:

- individual counselling;
- educational psychologist assessment;
- speech and language assessment;
- therapeutic educational programmes;
- enrichment days, including forest schools and team-building programmes.

The pupils also had opportunities to access multi-agency services, including drug and alcohol services, the youth offending team, probation services and our counselling service.

Outcomes

There were many lessons to be learnt throughout the project. Initially, schools sent pupils who had already received at least one suspension and the information provided was not always accurate. To address this, we began to observe all referred pupils in their schools, which enabled a correct placement to be offered. We also had to look at the dynamics of the pupils as the initial building we worked in was the ground floor of a terraced house with a small garden. After one year, the project was moved to a caretaker's bungalow, which was marginally better with some building modifications. On a Wednesday when all 16 pupils were together, we moved to a youth club site but we still needed to implement a clearer structure as many of the pupils struggled within the new group dynamics.

The main outcomes of the project were that the schools and the PRU were both accountable for the progress of the pupils who attended. There was a cohesive package of support and the opportunity to share outcomes which impacted on future developments with pupils with SEMH issues in both the mainstream school and the existing PRU offer. Did I achieve the 50 per cent reduction? By the time all the pupils reached the end of Year 11, only five pupils were permanently excluded, still not a number to celebrate but the impact for future practice was established.

Attendance and inclusion

If pupils do not attend school they do not learn and make progress. Getting pupils to attend school is the first priority for any school and it should start with what they perceive as inclusion. Attendance figures for the past few years have been declining, and since the Covid-19 lockdowns in 2020 and 2021 pupils have found it very difficult to return to school. They are feeling increasingly anxious around large groups of people and for those that experienced the death of a family member with whom they did not have the opportunity to see prior to their death, the attachment to their significant adult has become more entrenched. I had it described as pupils returning to their Reception years and the separation from their parent needed to be carried out again, but this time it was often with teenagers who could verbalise and demonstrate their refusal to go to school.

Currently it is reported by the Department for Education (2023) that there is a 22.6 per cent persistent absence rate across the country. Schools need to work in partnership to understand the reasons for this and how this can be addressed. Following the pandemic, many resources were developed to support the return of pupils in my local authority in partnership with a mainstream school's emotional well-being lead. We produced a package of support which was shared with all our secondary mainstream schools. The programme consisted of training for staff who were also vulnerable and a package of lessons to support the pupils each week when different emotions/anxieties may present themselves.

During the pandemic, the government's definition of vulnerable pupils included:

- pupils with an EHCP who have statutory rights and therefore agencies recognise and work within that framework;
- pupil premium children have additional funds and again there is a statutory expectation that this funding is spent and accounted for.

However, we all know that vulnerable learners are included in a much wider definition. All pupils who require additionality in mainstream schools or in PRUs/APs are vulnerable, and this list will grow significantly as we acknowledge families' personal circumstances changing, for example people losing their jobs and parental mental health needs increasing. My hope is that schools recognise that:

- EHCP pupils have visibility;
- pupil premium pupils have visibility;
- vulnerable learners with SEMH needs must have visibility.

REFLECTIVE TASK

Inclusive practices acknowledge that pupils' emotional well-being needs to be considered as a main precursor to positive behaviour and academic progress.

> *Emotional wellbeing is not simply the absence of mental illness but is a broader indicator of social, emotional and physical wellness. It reflects the interconnection of mind and body – physical health and mental health – and is concerned with the functioning of the whole person and the extent to which basic fundamental needs are met. It is influenced by the wider contexts within which a child or adult lives and the interaction between the individual, family, school / work and community.*
>
> (NICE guidance)

The NICE guidance on *Social and Emotional Wellbeing for Children and Young People* states that the above is based on the definition of well-being, which notes that a pupil should be able to:

- *[be] happy and confident and not anxious or depressed;*

- *[have] the ability to problem-solve, manage emotions, experience empathy, being resilient and attentive;*

- *[have] good relationships with others and not having behavioural problems – that is, not being disruptive, violent or a bully.*

Well-being also includes:

- *having a sense of meaning or purpose;*

- *being successful/having a sense of achievement;*

- *having a sense of control;*

- *giving and receiving attention and being validated.*

- In your school, how would you prioritise your inclusive practice using the need for well-being as described above?

Final thought

There are two statements which I feel conclude my feelings on inclusion.

> *Schools must be places that are welcoming and respectful, where every child has the opportunity to succeed. To ensure this is the case, they should understand how their policies impact differently on pupils depending on their protected characteristics, such as disability or race, and should give particular consideration to the fair treatment of pupils from groups who are vulnerable to exclusion.*
>
> (DfE, 2019, p 6)

I am always a bit suspicious of head teachers that start a conversation off by saying – we say 'What is the most important thing here?' and they say, 'We want our children to be happy'. I am always a bit suspicious of those heads. I am less suspicious of head teachers who say, 'I want our children to achieve'.

(Sir Michael Wilshaw, quoted in House of Commons
Education Committee, 2016, p 3)

I would argue the two go hand in hand. An emotionally literate school needs to keep its eye on academic achievement in order to remain emotionally literate – because everyone knows academic achievement increases life chances. Similarly, an academically orientated school needs to keep its eye on emotional well-being to maintain results and avoid burnout of young people. This is inclusion in unison.

KEY POINTS

- There is no 'I' in team.
- This is not 'rocket science'; inclusion embraces attachment, an acknowledgement of each pupil's needs and systems that ensure all pupils feel included. Remove the unneeded barriers.
- Exclusion does not help anyone, especially the child.
- Inclusion is a work in progress; it's a tough subject which needs powerful leadership.
- Schools own their inclusive practices. It needs to be personalised to your school, your pupils and your community.
- Inclusion is about partnership with the schools in your area, your PRU/AP provisions and the local authority. This ensures no pupil is left unsupported.

Further reading

Kotter, J (2006) *Our Iceberg Is Melting: Changing and Succeeding under Any Conditions*. London: Pan Macmillan.

References

Alternative Provision Quality Toolkit (2022) IntegratEd, hosted by the Centre for Social Justice. [online] Available at: www.centreforsocialjustice.org.uk/wp-content/uploads/2022/04/AP-Quality-Toolkit-2022.pdf (accessed 9 January 2024).

County Councils Network (CCN) Over 180 Children a Day Approach Councils for Special Needs Support as Local Authorities Warn That Government Reforms Will Not Stem the Tide. [online] Available at: www.countycouncilsnetwork.org.uk/over-180-children-a-day-approach-councils-for-special-needs-support-as-local-authorities-warn-that-government-reforms-will-not-stem-the-tide/ (accessed 28 February 2024).

Department for Education (DfE) (2019) *Timpson Review of School Exclusion*. [online] Available at: https://assets.publishing.service.gov.uk/government/uploads/system/uploads/attachment_data/file/807862/Timpson_review.pdf (accessed 9 January 2024).

Department for Education (2023) Pupil Attendance in Schools. [online] Available at: https://explore-education-statistics.service.gov.uk/find-statistics/pupil-attendance-in-schools/2023-week-16 (accessed 21 February 2024).

Department for Education (DfE) and Department of Health (DoH) (2017) *Transforming Children and Young People's Mental Health Provision: A Green Paper*. London: DfE and DoH.

Goddard, C (2019) Adverse Childhood Experiences: Building on the Strengths Within. *Children and Young People Now*, 23 September.

House of Commons Education Committee (2016) Oral Evidence: Purpose and Quality of Education in England, HC 650. 2 March. [online] Available at: https://committees.parliament.uk/oralevidence/5448/pdf/ (accessed 21 February 2024).

House of Commons Education Committee (2018) Forgotten Children: Alternative Provision and the Scandal of Ever Increasing Exclusions. [online] Available at: https://publications.parliament.uk/pa/cm201719/cmselect/cmeduc/342/342.pdf (accessed 21 February 2024).

Kotter, J (2006) *Our Iceberg Is Melting: Changing and Succeeding under Any Conditions*. London: Pan Macmillan.

Lost and Not Found (2023) The Centre for Social Justice. [online] Available at: www.noisolation.com/av1/case-studies (accessed 9 January 2024).

Shirley Valentine (1989) Directed by Lewis Gilbert [Film]. Paramount Pictures.

Twinkl (nd) Inclusion. [online] Available at: www.twinkl.co.uk/teaching-wiki/inclusion (accessed 28 February 2024).

Unicef (nd) Inclusive Education. [online] Available at: www.unicef.org/education/inclusive-education (accessed 28 February 2024).

Weale, S (2023) 180 Pupils a Day in England Given Special Needs Support Plan. *The Guardian*, 21 June. [online] Available at: www.theguardian.com/education/2023/jun/21/england-pupils-special-needs-support-plan-local-authority-deficits (accessed 9 January 2024).

5 Relationships within the PRU/AP and school partnerships

One of the strengths of my PRU was that there was a very clear understanding of me and what I could do. This did not happen overnight but took many years of developing school relationships. I had to be clear about what I could do and what I needed from my schools and often this proved really difficult. But as I was called 'tenacious' in one of my Ofsted inspections, people who knew me would expect nothing less. As new heads worked with me, I think they found me quite a challenge but I believe we became better colleagues for having those fierce conversations from the start. On one occasion after an altercation with one of the new heads he returned to his school and went into a colleague's office looking rather sheepish. He told her that he thought he was in trouble with me because he had done something in the referral panel he had just attended. By his own admission, he had worn a pink shirt he knew he felt confident in and he had turned the charm up to level 10. While speaking passionately about this pupil, he had sent a wink in my direction to which I replied, with my finger pointing, 'Don't you wink at me, sunshine'. I was not the kind of person to succumb to charm. We did laugh afterwards, but he has never lived this experience down. I promised if ever I wrote a book, I would share this story but not his name. He knows who he is.

Introduction

The work of a PRU or AP is linked by default to their partner schools and the relationships that develop. They are entrusting you with their pupils and that should come with responsibility. Many of the headteachers and senior leaders I have worked with care very much about where they are sending their pupils for additional support, but this is not always the case. The attitude of 'out of sight out of mind' was rarely a feature of those relationships and of the headteachers wanting a place for their pupils in my PRU. This was possibly due to the years of hard work I had put in to working with existing headteachers to remove those barriers and then, when new headteachers arrived, my reputation preceded me and the potential battle of accepting joint responsibility for their pupils' education was minimised. Most headteachers were confident that I would be able to make a difference to their pupils, and help them either return to their mainstream school or continue in further education.

Unfortunately, there still exists a significant number of headteachers and senior leaders who want the pupils who cause disruption to be moved out of their school. Historically, many heads did not want the pupil to return to their school. In some admission meetings, the school representative would say, '*They cannot come back to our school; they belong to you now*'. I would challenge this to the point where I would review the place and insist on further discussions outside of the meeting, which often resulted in the intended outcome that the pupil would return to their school after a period at the PRU. Can you imagine how that parent and pupil felt being told this for the first time in that meeting? Comments like '*If you do not agree to a move of school, I will have no option but to permanently exclude*' are still rife and I have experienced a number of occasions throughout my time as headteacher and executive headteacher in several authorities where the relationship between the PRU and the schools was poor. Some heads just want these pupils out of their school, and give little consideration to the quality of that placement or whether that pupil would have the opportunity to thrive. It still leaves me in awe that people who lead our profession, which is child centred, can have little regard for the needs of all the pupils under their care and feel more attuned or accountable to exam and school league tables and the ideals from Ofsted than the emotional stability of their pupils. Some will openly say, '*I feel like we are caught between academic results and the mental health stuff … and if push comes to shove…*' This feels so short-sighted. Anyone who has studied child psychology – again often missed in our teacher training programmes – would understand the connection between positive SEMH and academic progress and achievement.

The diagram below shows how the emotional needs of a pupil interact, link and impact on the academic achievements of a school.

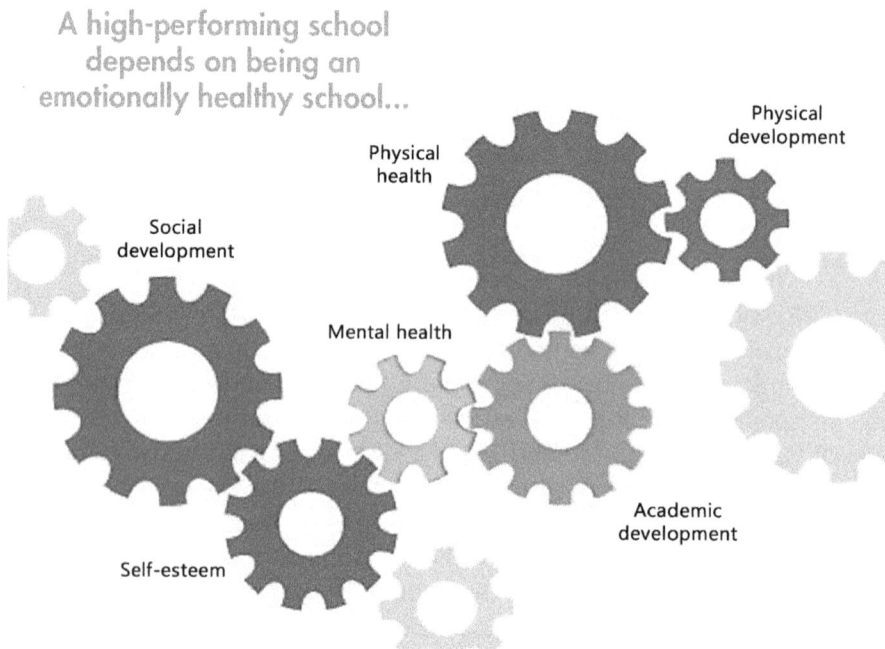

A high-performing school depends on being an emotionally healthy school...

Social development

Physical health

Physical development

Mental health

Self-esteem

Academic development

Figure 5.1 *How do the wheels turn in your school?*

This chapter explores the different partnerships that exist within the PRU and what can be beneficial and supportive to the final outcome, which is to help every pupil referred experience a quality-first education, however that might be constructed.

REFLECTIVE TASK

When I first became the headteacher, the pupils who were in the PRU had been there for up to 12 months. During that time, they had never made a visit to their school or had any contact with any of the teachers or other pupils. They returned to their mainstream school with little transition or reintegration. It felt like schools believed it was for us to change that pupil so they could walk straight back in. There was no consideration of how that pupil was feeling. I know that after every summer holiday I would feel anxious and not sleep for the last few days at the thought of the new academic year; what would my timetable be? What would the pupils be like? If I felt like this as an adult with coping skills, how could I expect a pupil to return to the school where their last experience had generally been fraught with anxiety, poor behaviour and unsupportive staff? It was basically unkind.

Therefore, I decided to establish a relational approach when working with schools. This was a way of interacting and communicating with my schools which embedded the core values of respect, inclusiveness, honesty, compassion, co-operation and humility. I needed everyone to see the pupil, not the behaviour or the actions which came from an emotional response to something that had been said or done towards them. A smile or a nod can make such a difference to how a pupil starts their school day.

- How do you feel at the start of a new academic year?
- How do you ensure that your staff are emotionally prepared for the year ahead on the first in-service day?

Who are the main partners?

During my years as a head of a PRU, my main partners were mainstream schools, the local authority and CAMHS/other health services. Social care came as an additional service if they were involved with a pupil or became involved once they were admitted to the PRU. What each partner wanted from the relationship needed to be considered but in essence we all had to have the same goal: to guarantee that the pupils referred not only received a good education but were provided with the best support to address those issues that were hindering their educational progress. I have collated the main requests of those partners.

Mainstream schools would like PRUs to see the following.

- A partnership with a clear understanding of entry and exit plans and regular communication in between these points. Both the PRU and the school need to be on the same page in terms of the 'end goal', which is to ideally return to the mainstream school, and the parts that both partners have to play. With this expectation, it is important that the pupil retains their home school identity – wearing their uniform and being part of school activities.

- Early assessment of any needs so that the pupil is aware of what their additional needs are and a clear plan made, communicated with the home school, so that they can prepare for reintegration as early as possible.

- Personalised intervention from specialists based in or from the PRU to help meet their needs, as these are less readily available in mainstream.

- Challenge and support from the PRU/AP, which does not give excuses for the pupil due to their needs but conveys high and realistic expectations. Pupils at the PRU should feel supported and able to succeed, but not that the PRU is 'easier' or 'softer' than mainstream; otherwise, transition back will be too hard.

- Staff at the PRU should validate and support mainstream processes so that the pupil knows what will be expected of them when they return.

- Transition support when the pupil is ready to return back to mainstream full time.

Local authorities would like to see the following.

- All PRUs and AP to offer a tiered approach with a clear strategy of what they can do.

- PRU/AP to assess pupils and have working knowledge on what the pupil's next steps should be and then support SEN to appropriately make EHCP referrals if necessary.

- Provide a range of interventions and recommendations which can be followed through on the pupil's return to mainstream school.

- Reduce permanent exclusion (PEX) and support suspensions at an earlier stage.

- Develop an outreach service to ensure pupils are supported both pre- and post placement.

CAMHS and other health services would like to see the following.

- Educational provisions to acknowledge the assessed mental health diagnosis and work with the CAMHS lead practitioner.

- To be part of health meetings so that they too can understand the needs/ constraints of a mainstream school.

- To joint manage the family expectations of the CAMHS service.

- To accept training and potential support of pupils with a range of health difficulties.

- To accept their support, especially when trying to return a pupil to mainstream school.

Leaders in PRUs and APs would like to see the following.

- Dual registration with joint partnership working.
- PRUs as educational centres and to be seen as that equal partner, that they are not the 'fluffy' friend.
- In partnership with schools to have shared corporate accountability for pupil outcomes and remove the 'blame' culture.
- For SEND, social care, admissions and social inclusion to work in partnership for the benefit of all the pupils.
- Good-quality referring information provided to support integration to the PRU and to provide a foundation for appropriate interventions to take place.
- That schools work in partnerships with PRUs and local authorities to develop funding systems that enable them to use provision flexibly and responsively while still supporting sustainability and growth of quality.

However, within every partnership, there has to be an equal and corporate responsibility to ensure that they can provide support and make a difference within an agreed time-frame. For many of the pupils I worked with, it was imperative that they had a speedy but supportive return to their mainstream school so that valuable learning was not lost. I also believed that pupils who could not attend their mainstream school for whatever reason needed to be provided with an educational placement that could meet their needs, either within the local authority or within a placement which was not too far away from their home, including a hospital placement.

Most PRUs and APs operate within a therapeutic model, which will provide a range of targeted, time-specific interventions. The debate as to how short or long these placements should be for is a matter for each PRU but it should never provide a 'sticking plaster' intervention. I remember interviewing a teacher for a position within my mental health team. She had to share how she would work with a pupil in school who was showing high levels of anxiety. She rolled up her sleeve to show her arm with both plasters and bandages on, and went on to say that when you removed a plaster it hurt and we all cringed as she swiftly removed hers. She then began to unwrap the bandage, very slowly and every so often a piece of paper fell out which showed an intervention that had been implemented and been successful. When the bandage was fully unfurled, there were no marks and this highlighted that good support and intervention, when removed, does not leave the pupil and family feeling abandoned – they have acquired the skills and knowledge to support themselves effectively. It also showed that the bandage could be put back on if needed and we did not have to go back to the beginning and start a new referral. This demonstrated the importance of time-limited but supportive interventions, especially for pupils with complex needs who require a degree of personalisation and sustained support. Therefore, placements can be short, medium or long term, but the aim and expected outcome is that every pupil can return and cope within a mainstream school.

In the document *Educational Excellence Everywhere* (DfE, 2016) the key messages about improving the outcomes of pupils who spent time in a PRU or AP were:

- partnerships with mainstream schools;
- agreed plan for the pupil's educational success;
- both specialist expertise and mainstream equivalent knowledge and skills;
- accountability;
- stability ahead of transition to appropriate post-16 provision;
- progress.

And the vision was to reform the AP system so that mainstream schools remained accountable for the education of pupils in the PRU/AP and were responsible for that commissioning. This was reiterated in the Timpson review (DfE, 2019) but is still not evident in the PRU-to-school relationship in many authorities.

Staff in a PRU/AP

Any staff working within a PRU/AP must, in my opinion, have experience of working within the mainstream school setting and I would personally never employ staff who had not worked in a secondary mainstream school for at least three years. If I was appointing within the primary sector, I would apply this prerequisite as well. I have often been asked why I insisted on this. The reason was simply that I was expecting my staff on occasions to challenge mainstream staff and provide basic training on how to support the pupils we were returning to their school. My staff needed to have a working understanding of what a mainstream school looked like and how frenetic they could be on occasions. No one likes to be told what to do by someone who has not got that knowledge. They would not be respected or listened to. To this end, as shared previously, my staff would spend CPD days in mainstream schools working within their particular specialism and in the behaviour support teams.

This hopefully helped them to be better-informed practitioners and to know what could work when reintegrating pupils. This is covered in greater depth in Chapter 6. This worked in many other ways. I established a reintegration programme for all my pupils and our educational psychologist agreed to deliver the module on emotional well-being. Our educational psychologist was an important partner for all our work. They would support any school or PRU assessments and complement these with further in-depth assessments and reports. This helped us to be better placed to provide effective interventions but more importantly they were our 'critical friend'. The opportunity for the educational psychologist to deliver a module proved beneficial for everyone. It became clear very quickly that theory and practice do not always work hand in hand. He said that he realised some of the things he would recommend to teachers in mainstream schools which were textbook interventions were not going to work. He felt his working practice was enhanced by delivering the module. This session was delivered to our Key Stage 3 pupils on a Friday as it helped them to set targets for the following week, but they were also tired and sometimes not very co-operative. He was ready for that extra glass of wine at the end of the working week!

Referral procedures

Referrals to the PRU have to be consistent and meet the admission criteria. It is important that all PRUs and APs are clear about what they can do and the expertise they may have within their teaching cohort. If these are not in place the PRU can be seen as a 'one size fits all' and the combination of the pupils admitted can become toxic.

When I first became head of the PRU, any other head or head of year could call me and we would discuss a pupil regarding whom I would then make the decision about what I could offer. Admission was arranged and we would then work with the school to provide further assessments and interventions. There was no local authority monitoring or involvement. They were informed when a pupil had been offered a place. This system did not show equity and the personal relationship I had with that staff member would often be the main precursor on whether a place was offered or not. Was I essentially confident the school would work with me and not change their mind once admission had been arranged? It had to change and a panel was developed, with schools, the local authority and educational psychologists contributing to any referral.

When schools decide they want to refer a pupil they should have internal processes to ensure that the right pupil is being referred. Whoever is asked to make the referral should arrange a meeting with all the staff members who work with that pupil to understand the purpose of the referral. This meeting should look at and collate the following information.

- What are the SEMH issues that have contributed to the referral being made?

- Can the school evidence what they have done to show that this is not a knee-jerk reaction but that the referral has been thought through and there has been a period of 'watchful waiting'? (Watchful waiting involves carefully monitoring areas of concern to see whether they improve or get worse. It's recommended because the majority of people who experience a 'dip' or 'low' in their mental health will get better within a few weeks without treatment.)

- Are there two 'plan, do, review' documents which show the interventions that have been put in place and why these have not worked? These are really important documents, especially if the school feels in the long term that an application for an EHCP assessment is needed.

- What are the pupil's current learning needs and is there any subject that the pupil is finding particularly difficult?

- What assessments, if any, regarding the pupil's SEMH needs have taken place?

- Are there currently any other agencies involved and, if so, what is their role and will they continue if the pupil is admitted to the PRU/AP?

- Are the parents/carers supportive of the referral and who has had this potentially difficult conversation?

- What are the school's expectations of the PRU and does the school accept joint responsibility?

- What practical support will the school make, for example transport to and from the PRU when reintegration is taking place?

- What are the re-entry arrangements for the pupil and what support will the school provide to continue with a supportive package of need?

Once the referral is received, who makes the final decision? I believe this should be via a multi-disciplinary panel with representatives from the local authority, secondary or primary heads, the educational psychologist and the head of the PRU/AP. In my experience, the educational psychologists I worked with would get very frustrated if a pupil was referred from a school they were working in and they had not had the opportunity to work with that pupil or at least had sight of the referral documentation. Educational psychologists are an important contributor to the assessment of need and for some pupils the referral to the PRU/AP may not even be needed.

CASE STUDY

I once received two referrals in the same meeting. I had previously worked with a Year 10 pupil who had cancer, and as I led the Home and Hospital Teaching Service, I had been providing the pupil with home tuition and liaising with the hospital medical staff. The pupil desperately wanted to take their GCSEs but it was not appropriate for them to return to their mainstream school.

The second referral was for a pupil who was in Year 8 and had moved into the authority. They were adopted and had been with their adoptive parents since a very early age and had received a diagnosis of schizophrenia. It was very unusual to diagnose this at such an early age and the CAMHS staff wanted them to be educated in the PRU before going to a mainstream school.

At the admissions panel, both cases were discussed but the suggestion of both pupils having a place was met with surprising responses. It was felt that the pupil with cancer should have a place but there were negative responses regarding the pupil with schizophrenia as they were concerned about how this pupil would present and impact on the other pupils. I decided that both were equally entitled to a place and both pupils started at the centre. The first pupil completed their GCSEs but sadly died the day after receiving their results. The other pupil suffered several episodes and was admitted into a psychiatric inpatient hospital on several occasions. However, the new mainstream school accepted the pupil and worked with CAMHS staff and ourselves. The pupil managed to maintain their school placement until the end of Year 11 and secured a place at college. The decision I made for both pupils to be given a place was the right one. Both met the criteria for a place at the PRU

---

and I feel it is important that our personal biases and perceptions do not impact on our decision making. While clear admission criteria are important, it is also important to remember the pupil behind the information and diagnosis.

REFLECTIVE TASK

- Using the information I have shared above, how do you make the decision to refer a pupil for a place at a PRU/AP?

- What documentation do you collate and who contributes to this process? Are you confident that a right referral has been made which is in the best interests of the pupil not the school?

- What does your school-to-PRU/AP partnership look like? What are the strengths and weaknesses and are there any changes you feel you need to make?

Admission arrangements

When it was agreed that my PRU was the best fit I would arrange an admission meeting with the pupil, parent/carer and school. All the parties had to be present to ensure that we were giving a clear message of unity. If there were other agencies involved, they would be invited to support the process. On admission, all my schools had to sign a contract. This included the following messages.

- A representative from the school will attend all planned review meetings and will endeavour to attend any emergency meetings should they be necessary. At least five working days' notice is required for a planned review meeting.

- The school would prioritise time with the school's educational psychologist (EP) if further assessment is required. We would allocate access to the counselling service and EP time from its own allocation as needed.

- The school and the PRU would jointly provide information for, or instigate, formal assessment if necessary.

- The pupil will remain dual registered between the PRU and the mainstream school. The pupil's name would not be removed from the PRU or school register without consultation.

- The PRU and the school would provide weekly information to support the pupil's attendance at both sites to support the final reintegration process.

- The school maintained the pupil premium monies and in consultation with the PRU would allocate these monies to support transition back into school or allocate alternative/additional services, eg taxis/vocational courses.

- The PRU would in consultation take responsibility to ensure that the pupil can be entered for external examinations. This would include marking of coursework, examination entry and identification of additional SEN support in line with any EHCP guidance.

- Any suspensions given by the school or PRU/AP would be in consultation with either headteacher and the school would in partnership make the necessary arrangements for the pupil to continue with their education at an alternative site.

- For all pupils entitled to a free school meal, the school will be billed half termly for the meals taken.

All my pupils were dual registered and would wear their own school uniform as I felt it was important that they maintained their own school identity, that they still felt 'attached' to their mainstream school, and this helped them to still belong. If they had been excluded, I would try very hard to ensure that the pupil had a new school identified and that the new school would attend the admission meeting. In agreement with the previous school and the new school, the pupil would wear a bland uniform which was only personalised once the reintegration process started.

I have always been very clear: my PRU was not a school; I ran a short-term provision and it was important that many of the school rules were continued. This included school uniform expectations and protocols regarding hair colour and body piercings. This simple but important guidance, especially if that pupil was returning to that school or any other school, showed that they had to follow established rules which I would reinforce with my pupils. I explained that even I had to do as I was told, which was to implement the rules of the government, local authority and their headteacher. This seemed to amaze the pupils as they thought I was the boss.

Establishing a new PRU/AP

In most local authorities, there are a range of established APs and PRUs and these are often tweaked to meet the needs of the pupils within that area. As with any other relationship, you have to establish ground rules – what will that partnership look like and what are their expectations of each other? This does not have to be complicated but should be clear.

However, there is a push for more PRUs/APs to be established by successful multi-academy trusts (MATs). These are my top ten tips to ensure that you can be successful and contribute to inclusion of the wider school community.

1. Sit down and write on a piece of paper your top five issues around SEMH in your school. Ask your school community to do the same and then collate the list.

2. Meet with the local authority SEN and inclusion leads. Where do they see the gap and what can they do to help you to set up the new provision?

3. Write the criteria for the provision which will be based on dual, not single, registration.

4. What staff do you need and can staff from across the MAT be seconded in the first instance to provide high-quality education?

5. What will the curriculum look like? You do not have to provide the full curriculum as specialist subjects can be accessed by the pupil in their mainstream school, but the provision should provide English, maths and science as a minimum, alongside practical subjects, for example, food technology and art. Other subjects offered could be the Duke of Edinburgh Award or programmes run by the Prince's Trust.

6. Identify the costs of running the PRU/AP. Do not miss out any hidden costs because someone has to pay for the things you might overlook, for example the maintenance of the building. What funding is available and how do you calculate your daily costs?

7. Agree an admissions contract which states clearly what is each other's responsibility but also have a very clear exit plan.

8. What will the provision look like on a daily basis and what do you want your pupils to achieve?

9. What support will you put in place for your staff to ensure they do not feel vulnerable and can leave at the end of the day feeling safe? Establish an end-of-day de-brief.

10. How can you use the referring school's expertise to complement your curriculum and school staff? For example, all my staff were attached to a mainstream school department where they could get their work assessed on their quality of marking to ensure that this was comparable to the mainstream school. This means that your staff are staying relevant and not making assumptions that they already have the right skills. Moderation of the PRU/AP staff is essential.

Establishing a flexible, meaningful curriculum for diverse needs

I have been lucky to work in many PRUs as the executive head and I was always amazed at the breadth of curriculum that they offered. It appeared that they thought they had to teach every subject offered within a mainstream curriculum. This in my opinion was unachievable as you had neither the staff nor the time to deliver an effective programme, and the pupils had been primarily referred for their SEMH needs and this needed priority in the first instance. This was why I felt it was important that my pupils spent time in their mainstream school every week. This is explained in more detail in Chapter 4.

The curriculum I established ensured that we not only addressed the pupils' learning needs but also focused on the reason they were with me, which was their SEMH needs. The curriculum I established included:

• core academic subjects, which included maths, science, English and computer science; within these subjects there were booster interventions and catch-up sessions, guided by the assessments we carried out on admission;

- additional academic subjects including art, humanities and food technology;
- the emotional and social curriculum which included personal, social, health and economic education (PSHE), emotional literacy, community counts and reintegration;
- our alternative curriculum which included Certificate of Personal Effectiveness (COPE), functional skills, forest schools and Duke of Edinburgh.

All my pupils left having achieved or with a better prospect of achieving both nationally recognised *and valid* qualifications. However, more importantly they had:

- improved mental health and increased emotional/social coping skills;
- a more positive experience of education;
- a successful transition back to mainstream education or a post-16 placement.

How can we support schools to be effective partners?

Many of the school leaders I spoke to had little idea of what they wanted my support to look like; in effect, they had a wish list, which in turn would help their staff to support pupils with SEMH more effectively. What I had to be clear about was that I did not have a magic wand. But they did say they wanted the following.

- The PRU to carry out a more rigorous assessment and identification of need, which would help support a pupil who had disengaged and who would be able to make a successful return to their mainstream school, special school or post-16 placement.
- To enable their schools to establish a package of support which could include their therapeutic input. This was not about individual sessions, but how the whole school workforce could change they way they worked with the pupils to make the school emotionally literate.
- To reintegrate the pupil back into their mainstream school; I will cover this in more detail in Chapter 6.
- To understand what training I could provide which will support the reintegration of pupils into mainstream schools and to provide appropriate and effective CPD, including mental health and behaviour training, child psychology and pedagogy, to strengthen whole school policies and procedures on how to support vulnerable learners.

It was within this list that we developed our CPD opportunities for mainstream school staff which would benefit everyone. I would provide placements for existing teacher and support staff to work in the PRU to help them develop their own behaviour management skills.

Our ambition was for staff to:

- develop an understanding of the most commonly diagnosed mental health conditions young people suffer with;

- be familiar with the screening strategies used in the identification of pupils with SEMH;

- understand methods of identifying and responding constructively to SEMH in young people;

- develop skills of liaison – consultation and partnership working;

- recognise the care pathways we had put in place and how these contributed to the reintegration of our pupils into their schools;

- reflect on the impact of personal values and attitudes on approaches to pupils with SEMH.

Our CPD programme was very comprehensive and staff could obtain qualifications in those courses, enabling them to be effective emotional well-being leads in their schools. Equally, as shared above, my staff would spend time in the mainstream schools. One way to ensure that the quality of education we provided was the same as a mainstream school was that all the teachers' marking was quality assured by mainstream staff. This was part of an effective CPD programme to make sure our assessment of work equalled that of a mainstream school.

Making a difference in initial teacher training

In 2012 I was asked to contribute to Charlie Taylor's initiative to deliver initial teacher training (ITT) in PRUs. The purpose of this was to enable new teachers to understand more about behaviour and how they could manage and sustain positive behaviour management in their classrooms. At that time many teachers were leaving the teaching profession, citing poor behaviour as one of their main reasons for making this decision. We had to try and stop this exit and I was really enthusiastic about being involved in this initiative. In my opinion this was an important initiative but it unfortunately has not been sustained fully as part of the teacher training programme. To address part of this issue, we delivered a mental health module in one of our local teaching schools, which proved to be highly successful. As we covered each module, we helped ITT students to create lesson plans to support pupils with ADHD, autism, anxiety and a range of other issues, which would help them include these pupils with additional needs into their classroom. In 2015, the Carter review of ITT spoke about the work we had been doing, stating:

> It provides an excellent grounding in many aspects of child development and well-being in a way that feeds into all other aspects of the ITT programme.

> Trainees, NQTs and recently qualified teachers (RQTs) who have experienced this course report a lasting impact in terms of knowledge, confidence and a much deeper awareness of the factors that can impact on pupil learning and wellbeing.
>
> (DfE, 2015, p 30)

The following recommendations in the review (DfE, 2015, pp 66–8) stated that all teacher training should include mental health and well-being.

- *Recommendation 1e: Child and adolescent development should be included in all age phases within a framework of core ITT content.*

- *Recommendation 1f: Managing pupil behaviour should be included in a framework for ITT content, with an emphasis on the importance of prioritising practical approaches throughout programmes.*

- *Recommendation 1g: Special educational needs and disabilities should be included in a framework for ITT content. This should prepare all new teachers to support SEND in their classrooms, providing a solid grounding in the most pertinent issues and setting an expectation for on-going high quality professional development.*

- *Recommendation 10: Wherever possible, all ITT partnerships should build in structured placements for trainees in special schools and mainstream schools with specialist resourced provision – ideally, trainees should have opportunities for assessed placements.*

For all teachers, I feel it is imperative they have an understanding of SEMH and are not frightened of working with these pupils.

Post-16 transition

I did not expect the Year 11 pupils who completed their GCSEs at the PRU to gain the same number of passes as the pupils in mainstream schools, but I believed this should not hinder their opportunities of gaining a place in any post-16 college. To ensure no barriers existed, my centre developed an effective post-16 transition and spent time in the colleges working with the college leads to promote the positives our pupils would bring to their college. Through this understanding of the aims of the PRU, the pupils could follow A level courses which they were capable of passing.

However, there was unfortunately a pattern of pupils moving to college but often not completing their courses. This needed to change and better support systems on transition needed to be established. I worked with my staff to improve relationships with the colleges, establishing links for the pupils and ensuring that pertinent information, with the permission of parents and pupils, was shared with key people.

The transition process established consisted of several steps.

- A mini open day event – the majority of pupils attending the PRU felt unable to attend a college open event where hundreds of pupils and parents would be visiting the college at the same time. The colleges provide a mini event for our pupils, giving them the opportunity to meet key staff, often including the principal, and to have a tour of the college. On some occasions ex-pupils from the PRU met with the pupils to share their college experiences.

- Prior to allocating places, colleges would liaise with the PRU regarding pupils' needs. Relationships were such that colleges would be led by the PRU's recommendations.

- Prior to starting college, the pupils met with a member of staff from the learning support team accompanied by a member of staff from the PRU to discuss any support which could be beneficial on transition. The support could include such things as a red exit card/a blue *'don't ask me'* card, a weekly one-on-one well-being support session with a key person and use of a quiet space when necessary.

- College staff would often visit the PRU prior to the summer break to further establish relationships and answer any worries or concerns.

- Once the pupils started at college, a member of staff from the PRU would visit the colleges each week for the first half term and arrange a drop-in with the pupils – this allowed the pupils the opportunity to air any concerns with a trusted adult who could then help them to negotiate the new relationships with staff at the college. More often than not, by the end of the half term the pupils were not attending the drop-in sessions – the PRU's work was done! The pupils had spread their wings.

- With these relationships in place, the colleges then began to contact the PRU with any concerns regarding pupils and, wherever we could, staff offered support and advice, often going into college to support meetings with parents. This was often all that was needed to get things back on track.

With all this established, the pupils experienced a far more positive college experience and have gone on to great things. A true testament that time spent in a PRU or AP to address specific needs at certain points in a pupil's development definitely shouldn't hinder their opportunities for success in the future.

Creating a school to PRU/AP checkpoint service

No school or PRU should exist as an island. We can all learn from each other and I have always been a firm believer that you should not waste time reinventing new tools. If there is good work happening in your school for pupils with SEMH then you should share that practice and collectively a local authority or MAT will become stronger. One of the best meetings we established was a checkpoint service where we invited all our named emotional well-being leads in primary, secondary and post-16 colleges to share what they were doing and the resources they had found. Each half term, a colleague would be invited to talk about any specific areas where we could develop support in our schools. The educational psychologist and CAMHS lead were important members. The purpose of establishing the checkpoint service was to:

- provide a 'very early intervention' service for schools in which pupils regarded as a cause for concern regarding their SEMH could be discussed anonymously to look at 'what next';

- help the group to develop a strategy bank created with ongoing consultative support from my PRU through half-termly meetings;

- identify a range of training in consultation with schools which will support and empower your mainstream schools to provide a range of Tier 1/2 therapeutic interventions to support assessment of need and further referral to specialist services;

- develop specific accredited training programmes for colleagues in schools, which would train up staff to deliver Tier 1 support, for example bereavement and loss and trauma-informed practice.

What can schools do differently?

I know of many schools who are trying to change the school experience for their more vulnerable learners. They recognise that they have to do something 'different' and that one size fits all is an outdated concept within our mainstream schools. Change does not have be expensive, but a few tweaks within the existing staffing structure and curriculum would ensure all your pupils want to come to school. Heads could ask all their staff the question, 'What do you teach?' If they say their subject area, they should be concerned; the right answer would be, 'I teach children and to be confident that every teacher should contribute to the behaviour management and SEN within their school. It is not someone else's job'. The quote and the examples provided demonstrate the need for teachers to not only know their subject but to recognise the role they have for every pupil.

> Sometimes it can be difficult to go on believing in another person when that person seems not to believe in him or herself. Yet one of the greatest gifts a teacher can offer a student is the refusal to accept the student's poor self-concept at face value, seeing through it to the deeper, strong self that exists within if only as a potential.
>
> (Branden, 1995, p 211)

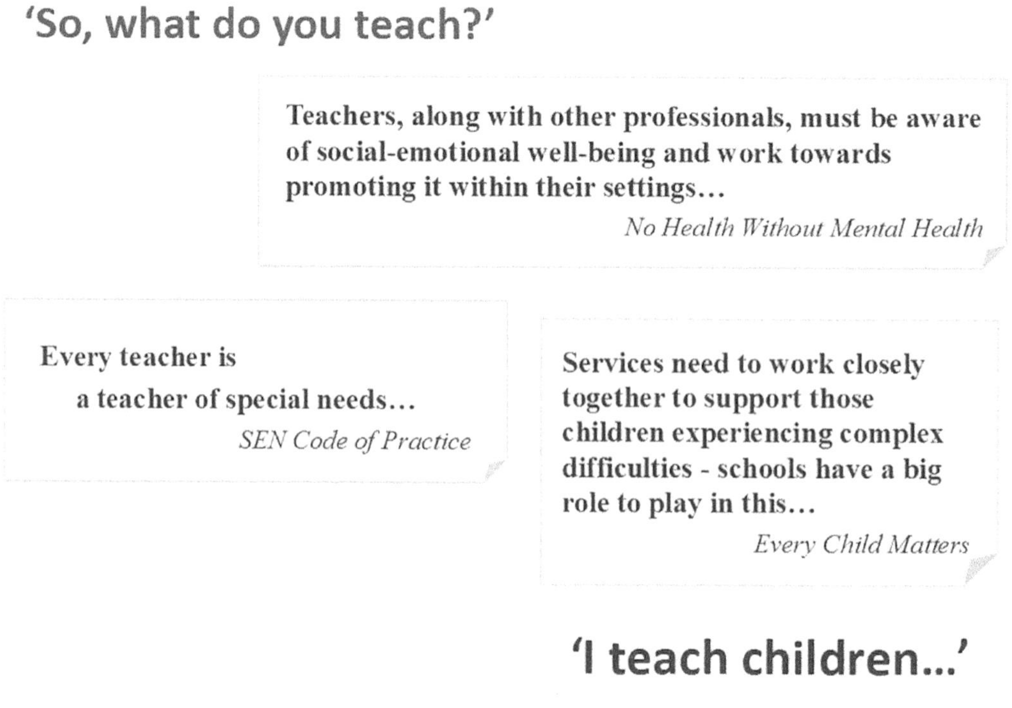

'So, what do you teach?'

Teachers, along with other professionals, must be aware of social-emotional well-being and work towards promoting it within their settings...

No Health Without Mental Health

Every teacher is a teacher of special needs...

SEN Code of Practice

Services need to work closely together to support those children experiencing complex difficulties - schools have a big role to play in this...

Every Child Matters

'I teach children...'

Figure 5.2 *How do your staff see their role in your school?*

REFLECTIVE TASK

Our childhood memories are dominated by our relationships, and events in which those relationships played out.

Our childhood memory is not dominated by learning objectives, worksheets, Kagan-style discussion groups and three-point marking feedback. Not that this is unimportant or readily dismissed – but you have to be clear about what ultimately drives such things. Schools should be seen as a safe space where children can thrive.

- Try to think of two to three standout memories from your time at school. These could be memories of lessons *or* memories of people and one-off events.
- What effect did they have on your future aspirations?

Final thought

At my fourth inspection the inspector said, '*This is a place for learning*'. He also called me an anomaly and according to *Roget's Thesaurus* this can mean:

- non-conformance;
- strangeness;
- dissent;
- awkwardness;
- infraction of the rules;
- breach of practice.

Many of my colleagues would agree with this but it can equally mean:

- individuality;
- uniqueness;
- special case.

And I believe that PRUs and APs are very special places for very special children and young people. Mainstream schools have an important role to play in ensuring PRUs and APs do their job to the best of their ability.

KEY POINTS

- There is no 'I' in team.
- This is not rocket science – schools and PRUs working in partnership should be the same as any other partnership developed by a mainstream school.
- All MATs should consider establishing their own PRU to ensure that pupils within their family schools continue within that family.
- Work with the PRU or AP in your area to ensure that it provides for your pupils and complements the work you are doing within your mainstream school to promote inclusion.
- Do not close the doors on these pupils. They will enrich your school, especially when you facilitate the opportunity for them to achieve their personal aspirations.
- Permanent exclusion does not solve anyone's problem and it marks a pupil for their future pathways. Do you have the right to do that?

Further reading

Department for Education (DfE) (2021) *Responsibility-Based Models of Decision Making, Funding and Commissioning for Alternative Provision: Research Report*. [online] Available at: www.gov.uk/government/publications/commissioning-models-for-alternative-provision (accessed 9 January 2024).

References

Branden, N (1995) *The Six Pillars of Self-Esteem*. New York: Random House.

Department for Education (DfE) (2015) *Carter Review of Initial Teacher Training*. [online] Available at: www.gov.uk/government/publications/carter-review-of-initial-teacher-training (accessed 9 January 2024).

Department for Education (DfE) (2016) *Educational Excellence Everywhere*. [online] Available at: www.gov.uk/government/publications/educational-excellence-everywhere (accessed 9 January 2024).

Department for Education (DfE) (2019) *The Timpson Review of School Exclusion: Government Response*. [online] Available at: https://assets.publishing.service.gov.uk/government/uploads/system/uploads/attachment_data/file/800676/Timpson_review_of_school_exclusion__government_response.pdf (accessed 9 January 2024).

6 Reintegration with meaning

As previously shared, when I first became the headteacher of my PRU most pupils did not return to or visit their mainstream school until the completion of their 12-month placement. It was a cruel way to reintegrate and that is why I have always promoted reintegration from day one. The only exception to this process was when we received Year 11 pupils, and we made the decision that it would be best for them to attend only the PRU. I have always been lucky that my pupils would return and let me know how they were doing. On one occasion, one of my pupils came to say she was going to university but it had taken her an extra year as when she transitioned to her post-16 college, she found it difficult to integrate with her peers. I asked her if we could have done anything better to help, to which she replied:

> You should have sent us back to our mainstream school, not full time but that would have helped us to get used to the large crowds and the demand of a mainstream college.

On reflection, I realised how this would have helped and I immediately changed the Year 11 offer to include part-time attendance of our Year 11 pupils at their mainstream schools. Fortunately, most schools saw the advantages of the changes I implemented.

Introduction

Schools suspend and exclude pupils every day. For those suspended they return to their school within a fixed period of time and the suspension itself is seen as the punishment. Pupils are often expected to learn and address their issues independently and know what to do to ensure that they are not suspended again. Suspensions are a punitive act and most of us would hope that when those pupils do return, a package of support is put in place to help move them forward. In reality, this is not normal practice and therefore many pupils receive further suspensions and ultimately a permanent exclusion, with schools saying the pupils did not learn from their mistakes. But how can pupils learn if their mistakes are not discussed and supportive strategies are not put in place to help them change, including their teachers adopting new ways of engaging with them? Those pupils receiving a permanent exclusion very rarely return to another school, especially if it is their second exclusion, and will be sent to and remain in a PRU or AP for a long time. This chapter focuses on good reintegration, which the PRU/AP and schools should manage collectively.

What is reintegration?

If partnership working and placement at a PRU or AP is well planned and organised, reintegration is not seen as an 'add-on'. It is part of the educational offer of support for the pupil, their family and the school.

If schools implement behaviour policies that are supportive, pupils are more willing to return to their mainstream school as they know poor behaviour will be challenged. When I created the PRU timetable with my staff, we had to be mindful of staff that would be needed to support the pupil's return to their school. To that end we created a reintegration lead whose main job was to liaise with schools and the pupil's family to ensure that everyone knew what was happening each week. Historically, all my teaching staff had spent at least one day a week in schools, observing pupils and supporting those that needed help prior to a referral. With demands on the teaching staff's time, this role was no longer cost-effective. We needed schools to be our gatekeeper prior to referrals and our support staff in the first instance would be asked to provide in-school support to ensure the reintegration process was successful. However, every member of the PRU team, including myself, had to be prepared to provide support in school. No one was excluded from this role. The construction of the timetable to enable this support was difficult and lesson planning at times could be a nightmare.

Our method of reintegration evolved over many years but there were some pre-requisites that I needed to put in place.

- Dual registration – all our pupils were dual registered, including those that had been permanently excluded who were allocated a new school on admission.

- Contract of agreement with schools – on admission the schools had to sign an agreement to show what they and we would do to support the process.

- Pupil premium – if a pupil was in receipt of pupil premium, this was not given to the PRU but maintained by the school and was spent in agreement with me to ensure it supported the reintegration process. We used this money for taxis to transfer the pupil between the school and the PRU, or to provide additional teaching or support staff allocation.

Schools' approach to SEMH and reintegration: my process

When a pupil was referred to the PRU, the school knew that the pupil would be dual registered and accepted that the pupil would attend within the first two weeks on an agreed package of support. Parents and pupils had to accept that this was part of the placement offer, and that there was no negotiation to stop this happening. Some parents thought that once their child was admitted, their school attendance would decline but I always made it clear this would not be the case. Part of our work at this point was to provide the parents with support and try to allay any anxieties they had.

Placement at the PRU was time limited. In the admission meeting, the time was to be spent at the PRU with key milestones and meetings agreed. The exit criteria were set at this meeting but I was realistic; I was working with people, not a system, and it had to have some flexibility built into it. Key Stage 3 pupils attended the PRU full time for the first two weeks and they then increased their time in school. Their placement was for a maximum of two terms and in the third term, we would provide support and the parents always knew that they could call us if there was a problem developing. Year 10 pupils attended for three days each week for a maximum of one term as it was imperative that they attended lessons in their chosen GCSE subjects so as to not fall behind their peers. In Year 11, pupils chose a GCSE we could not offer and would attend all those lessons in school to continue with that GCSE. In this way, the pupils all felt some attachment to their mainstream school.

Preparation for the return was agreed with the pupil. For some the first step was to simply get into a staff member's car and drive to the school and sit in the car park. The next visit could be a teacher they knew coming to the car and saying hello and the third visit could be walking around the school during lessons with a map of the school and traffic lighting the areas that they found most difficult. From this point, we could begin to create a personalised plan of support. As part of the initial assessments we carried out, pupils would fill in a School Stress Survey, which was a visual document where they could rate their school day from getting up in the morning to going to bed at night. This helped my staff to focus on the trigger points throughout the school day and ensure additional support could be provided at those key times.

Deciding on the lessons the pupils would attend could be difficult, especially if the school believed the pupils needed to be in certain lessons. However, with discussion we could identify and demonstrate that pupils accessing lessons they enjoyed with staff they trusted actually supported the reintegration process and ensured their overall success. When the pupils were in the PRU, we built in personal study sessions so they could catch up on work they had missed in school or at the PRU.

As the pupils' attendance at school began to increase, the reintegration lead would meet with specific school staff to share the progress the pupil was making and discuss amendments to their timetable and what support we believed needed to be in place. We needed to share how they could get the best out of the pupil and we would often shed new light on the pupil's needs, how they felt in school and the difficulties they perceived, and be their voice.

Each week, we would email weekly reports about the progress the pupil had made with targets that we had set together for them to achieve in school. This was a reciprocal arrangement, with schools emailing us with their report of pupils' progress. Any difficulties they had would then be the focus of the PRU staff, who prioritised these difficulties in preparation for the next attendance session.

All our pupils were given a pack of cards which they could use with their school's agreement. These cards covered the areas the pupils knew they would find difficult in class and would say the following.

- Please do not single me out with a question.
- I don't understand what you have asked me to do.
- I need a time out for five minutes as I am feeling anxious.
- I can leave the lesson a few minutes before the bell so I can get down the corridor before it becomes too busy.
- I need help but if I put my hand up, I am drawing attention to myself.
- I have permission to arrive at morning registration late so I can catch a later bus.
- I can eat my lunch at an agreed space rather than in the school canteen.

The car journey

We found that when transporting the pupils to their schools, it was an opportunity for the pupils to talk about how they were feeling. Sitting in the car, with no eye contact, the pupils felt more confident and less threatened to be able to share their thoughts. The member of staff could talk through what they were going to do and what plans had been agreed and put in place. It was an opportunity to help the pupils de-stress. The member of staff could also go through 'what if' scenarios so the pupil felt more confident about what would happen. While the car journey was important, it also highlighted to staff that we needed more time to prepare the pupil. To this end we developed a reintegration programme which became part of our curriculum. There were seven units developed to address many areas of SEMH difficulties our pupils may experience. I believed that through this programme their self-esteem and confidence would improve.

Aims of the reintegration programme

- To identify each pupil's SEMH difficulties, which had prevented or contributed to their difficulties in accessing their mainstream school.

- To enable each pupil to understand theirs and others' behaviour within an educational setting and provide them with skills which would enhance their existing coping strategies.

- To enable the pupil to enter into and sustain mutually satisfying personal relationships.

- To ensure that the school, while supporting learning, acknowledges the emotional difficulties which may affect the pupils' learning.

Overview

- The programme was comprised of seven units, taught over one academic year.

- There were approximately five sessions in each unit.

- The units could be delivered in any order, dependent upon the group's needs.

- Each session began with a plenary which included all pupils filling in an Emotions Log and at the end of the session they filled in a Learning Log.

- Throughout the programme there were a range of assessment tools used to guide and inform planning.

Units of work

- Dealing with our emotions.

- Developing communication skills.

- Organisation.

- Social skills, including anger management.

- Physical well-being, including healthy eating.

- What is mental health?

- Peer group interaction.

The final hurdle

The final hurdle was always at the end of the placement. I believed that during a pupil's time at the PRU we had addressed their difficulties, and throughout their reintegration we had the opportunity to revisit and address those issues that were difficult to resolve. But I could not allow this to stop or prolong the process of reintegration. Ultimately, the pupil had to leave us; what we had to ensure was that we had given the school their 'toolbox' of need. With the school's input we would produce a personalised menu of support. Some of the things we would implement were to:

- establish the pupil's 'safe place', which could be the library, reception, pastoral room or SEN room;

- produce a personalised learning plan (PLP);

- produce an end of placement report;

- create a pupil passport which showed the pupil's strengths and weaknesses which may trigger support needed for their SEMH needs.

Key Stage 4

I have spoken previously about our Year 11 placement, and I firmly believe that the changes we made had a profound impact on the success of our pupils. The majority were proud that they had been able to return to their home school and face some of their demons. They re-engaged with their learning and it supported their post-16 transition when they would again have to face some of those pupils who had contributed to their feelings of aloneness and anxiety.

Post-16

Post-16 transition was very important to ensure that the work we had put in place worked well. Our Year 11 pupils had not fully returned to their mainstream school and the thought and detail we put into a school return had to be replicated in the colleges. Fortunately, we built up very good relationships with post-16 colleagues so that we could implement:

- college visits outside the general open day/evening sessions;

- arrangements to talk and meet with the admissions staff;

- arrangements to attend and support at admission meetings because often the parents could not do this;

- negotiations of the course the pupils wanted to follow as the pupils could achieve six GCSEs and not always in the subjects they wanted to pursue;

- in the first half term, a member of my staff would be at the colleges for a certain time each week so that they could meet with staff and chat about how things were progressing.

Reintegration of permanently excluded pupils

There is a feeling that pupils who have been permanently excluded should stay at the PRU or AP allocated to them for their remaining time in education. I do not believe that this should be the case. SEMH does not start in Year 7 and end at Year 11, yet many of these pupils once they leave school move on to have a good career and achieve their potential. School has been their Achilles heel and if they are not allowed to go back into a school and have a positive experience, that feeling of negativity will stay with them.

We all make mistakes, but we all deserve second chances. For some pupils, to stay at a PRU for two years may be what they need. The PRU can meet their needs but if pupils are not given the opportunity to return to a mainstream school, I feel we are doing them an injustice and I would ask that all schools and local authorities build in those opportunities. They are possible.

> *While adverse experiences in early childhood can cause children to develop maladaptive ways of viewing themselves and the world, the brain remains plastic, and it is possible to over-write pathways learned in adversity with new ways of thinking and reacting. However, this does not happen by magic, and it does not happen overnight.*
>
> (Brooks, 2020, p 54)

Pupils' approach to reintegration

Most of my pupils said on their first visit that they never wanted to return to their school or in fact any school again. Schools held a raft of negative emotions and they felt it was just too hard to return. PRUs and APs can engage pupils fairly quickly due to their size and the skills of their staff. The pupils attach quickly and want to stay. But the small PRU environment is not real life. They will eventually have to work and be alongside their peers and it should be one of the main objectives of the PRU to facilitate this. That's not to say we can meet their needs and they will be happier here. When I have spoken to pupils who have been permanently excluded, they will say on reflection that they would still like to go back to school and be with their friends, and those opportunities need to be available. If we never challenge or put those pupils back into that environment they find so scary, how do we know that they will never change and succeed? It always seemed a bit arrogant to me that PRU leaders had this belief that they were the rescuers of lost lives.

REFLECTIVE TASK

In Chapter 4, I shared the five PCs. Here is the definition in more detail.

1. **Positive contribution**: Our students will want to engage and participate in their learning provided by excellent teaching, which is underpinned by excellent professional development.

2. **Positive communication**: Through removing inherent barriers to learning, our students will realise their academic and personal potential and will be able to communicate effectively to make exceptional achievement possible.

→

3. **Positive creativity**: By adopting a holistic approach and providing appropriate therapeutic interventions we will promote each individual's creativity, which will help them flourish and grow.

4. **Positive co-operation**: Through an acceptance of individual needs and acceptance of specialist input, SEMH difficulties will be addressed to enable all young people to move along their educational and personal pathway. We do not accept excuses or make any either.

5. **Positive confidence**: Our students will develop 'mental toughness' by building their resilience and fulfilling their academic aspirations, feeling valued by themselves and their community.

- Looking at your school ethos, is there anything here that you would challenge and what would you change?

CASE STUDY

Several years ago, I was admitting a Year 7 boy. He had started at his secondary school but on an outdoor activity he became unwell and the other pupils were not particularly kind. He refused to return to school. He became increasingly challenging and abusive towards his parents and they did not know what to do. On his admission, he refused to speak to me and sat underneath the table calling me names and shouting at his parents. I informed him that the meeting would continue but I would like him to listen. He became so angry and literally smashed up my office, turning over bookshelves and chairs. His parents were mortified; his mother cried and felt she was the 'bad parent'. I said this does not matter, but if they could bring him to the centre the next day again just for a visit we would start again. His transition to the PRU took a term and eventually he attended full time and was confident in his learning and with his peers. A return to his original mainstream was not feasible so another school was allocated via the local authority and secondary headteachers' panel. We decided to allocate one member of staff to support this as he would still run away and hide when his anxiety levels became too high, but after a term he transitioned fully into the school. He went on to be head boy, was part of the rugby team, and achieved his GCSEs, A levels and a university placement. I remember once going into that school for a meeting and when he saw me, he said, '*What are you doing here? I'm doing really well*'. I replied, '*I know, I'm coming to see someone else but how good you look*'. He beamed.

This is an example of a reintegration programme we initiated for one of our Key Stage 3 pupils.

Table 6.1 *Example reintegration programme*

	Current offer	Case study
PREPARATION	Curriculum offer • Core subjects in small groups. • Enrichment activities/D of E which promote positive social interaction and team working. • Emotional well-being sessions – targeted interventions to address needs identified by well-being assessments carried out on entry. • Careers sessions. • Therapeutic art. • Reintegration lessons – to prepare for return to school. • Mainstream school attendance from date of admission.	• Accessed the full curriculum. • Gained confidence to participate more fully by being in smaller groups. • Well-being sessions targeted social interaction and self-esteem. • Attendance improved. • Great deal of work also carried out with parents, especially the pupil's mum, to address her anxieties and distress; this would also have a positive impact on the pupil.
	Assessments • Baseline assessments in core subjects on entry and every half term to assess academic progress throughout the placement. • TAPS (Approach to Tasks/Adults/Peers/Self) half-termly. • Emotional assessments on entry and exit: PASS (Pupil attitude to self and school), Resiliency scales, SDQ (Strengths and Difficulties Questionnaire) – these help to inform the intervention work for each pupil, both formal and informal.	• Links with CAMHS and school mental health team to carry out CBT and suicide risk assessments on a regular basis.

→

Table 6.1 (Cont.)

	Current offer	Case study
	Interventions • Feedback from mainstream school and own pupils' responses in reintegration lessons inform specific pieces of work for individual pupils during the reintegration process.	• CBT sessions. • Mental Health Practitioner (MHP) liaised with mainstream school.
MECHANISMS	Pupil eligibility • Following assessments and intervention, the pupil is deemed able to increase access to a mainstream provision both academically and emotionally.	• Pupil wanted to and attempted to return to referring mainstream school. Pupil's mum keen initially for her to do so. Previous difficulties arose very quickly so 'fresh start' agreed.
	Allocation to a new school • If the mainstream placement has broken down to such an extent that returning is impossible. • PEX. • Need a fresh start.	• New mainstream school worked closely with recommendations from the PRU and slow integration was achieved, allowing the pupil to now access a full and varied curriculum and make new friendships. • CPD provided for mainstream school staff to enable transition.
	Requirements for reintegration achievement • Pupil to be able to access the curriculum and feel safe and secure in the environment – this may often require the mainstream school to implement necessary adjustments for the individual – all outlined on passport and discussed with the mainstream school link and teaching staff as and when possible.	• CAMHS and other services involved support process, eg school age plus worker to transport to mainstream school.

Table 6.1 (*Cont.*)

	Current offer	**Case study**
SUPPORT	Welcome • Mainstream school is involved with the pupil throughout their placement – admission meeting/reviews/final meeting. They are expected to liaise with the PRU weekly to inform of issues arising when in school so that these can be addressed before the next visit. PRU informs the school of any issues and progress made to ensure transparency and full understanding of need.	• Pupil referred through Fair Access Protocols (FAP), chaired by a secondary head and agreed by local authority and all secondary heads. • New mainstream school was involved in referral discussions and meeting with parents and pupil in school to discuss historical issues and what they could do – transparency and realistic aspirations agreed.
	Input • Historically, outreach support was available throughout the reintegration but resources now limit this and it is dependent on need. • A positive from this is that school staff are supported and advised by PRU staff so that they can offer the necessary support 'in house'.	• Support for this pupil was provided by PRU staff initially and in the first six weeks at the school's request. • School staff worked collaboratively with the PRU to implement strategies which had worked in Pendlebury.

REFLECTIVE TASK

- Using the previous case study, reflect on how you reintegrate your pupils.
- What do you put in place to ensure their return is a positive experience and that ultimately the number of suspensions and exclusions in your school reduces?

Final thought

Successful reintegration is possibly one of the most rewarding feelings you can have. If you don't get reintegration right, pupils will stop attending school and by default become part of the lost generation: those children that do not go to school for whatever reason and become lost in a system. It is our duty to ensure that we help pupils to return to their mainstream schools with the skills and competencies to be successful and to have ownership of their own future.

KEY POINTS

- There is no 'I' in team.

- This is not rocket science – the next steps after the PRU/AP placement have to be planned. Entry and exit into the PRU needs to be planned; the next steps are not something you determine months into the placement if a smooth transition is to be achieved.

- The best thing my pupils ever said to me was, '*Please go away Miss, I don't need your help anymore. I can do this on my own*'. I beamed.

Further reading

Holt-White, E and Cullinane, C (2023) *Social Mobility: The Next Generation. Lost Potential at Age 16*. London: The Sutton Trust.

The Centre for Social Justice (2022) *Lost but Not Forgotten: The Reality of Severe Absence in Schools Post-Lockdown*. London: The Centre for Social Justice.

Reference

Brooks, R (2020) *The Trauma and Attachment Aware Classroom*. London: Jessica Kingsley Publishers.

7 Multi-agency working and the importance of positive mental health provision for all

Question: How many times do you hear yourself saying *'I'm expected to be a social worker, health professional, parent and teacher?'*

Answer: Every day, and why? Because we think we are the only ones who will get the job done!

As headteacher of a PRU, I often had to embrace different roles to ensure that the families and pupils I met were given what I believed to be the best service. When I set up our multi-agency mental health team, I was not always prepared to listen to other agencies and what they felt was the right approach. I had to learn to listen and accept that I needed to follow their advice. A hard lesson but one I came to value as by working in a multi-disciplinary way, you are more empowered to do the right thing.

Introduction

Have you ever been sitting in a meeting and heard someone say, *'It's not my fault, it's yours!'*? In my opinion this is about creating real barriers to multi-agency working.

Barriers real or perceived are only put up by yourself because you are fearful of working outside your 'comfort zone' and you choose not to listen, change and learn. In theory, multi-agency working should be one of the easiest things to achieve. A group of like-minded individuals sitting around a table, with one formal objective and the means to achieve this within their capabilities. In practice it is never quite that easy. This chapter looks at examples of how multi-agency working can enhance the support provided for pupils in schools to ensure that they are safe and have the tools to remain in school and make progress.

Multi-agency working

Unfortunately, in today's society, there is a strong 'blame culture' where if things go wrong, we have to be able to identify an individual or a process that has contributed to or caused that failure. This seems to make us feel better and provides a solution. In reality, we all have a corporate responsibility for failure as well as success and we should be confident enough and supported sufficiently to take this on.

Therefore, while we sit in meetings, smiling and communicating, underneath there is a personal agenda of how we can watch our own backs and ensure we do not become the scapegoat. The image I present seems extreme and I do not think that anyone would wittingly enter into multi-agency working with this thought at the forefront but I do believe it is a precursor to some of our actions.

How many meetings have you been in where one of the professional agencies either has not turned up or feels there is *'no role for us here'*?

I propose two potential reasons for this response.

1. If you don't turn up, the group cannot allocate your service and confirm your level of involvement. If you do, you have time to delay and pontificate about whether you should be involved.

2. You turn up, set the benchmark high to suit yourself as you know the mechanisms within your profession will not be able to deliver – you save face before you get too involved.

Good multi-agency working is hard work. Fact. It requires each individual to be prepared to change their mindset and to accept the corporate responsibility for each other. You listen to others' points of view and opinions, you discuss your thoughts and fears openly, and together you set up a plan of action with each one of you accepting your role, while at the same time accepting collective responsibility for success or failure.

The document *Every Child Matters* (DfE, 2003) demanded that agencies work together, pooling resources and expertise to take an integrated approach. The White Paper *Back on Track* (DfE, 2008, p 5) also recommended that:

> *There should be better partnership working between alternative provision, other parts of the education sector and other agencies and services working with young people to facilitate early intervention and ensure an integrated approach to meeting the young person's needs.*

The *Special Educational Needs and Disabilities (SEND) and Alternative Provision (AP) Improvement Plan* (DfE, 2023) states:

> *The new National Standards and local partnerships and plans will provide clarity in the system and encourage people to work together, but we know there is a need for stronger incentives and better enforcement for local areas, including providers, to meet statutory duties.*
>
> (DfE, 2023, p 73)

By taking this integrated approach you move away from 'teacher knows best' to empowering young people to be informed, motivated and skilled to make good choices. After all, the opposite of integration is disintegration and it is your role to prevent this happening to your most vulnerable young people.

Joshua Freedman in his book *Handle with Care* (1998) states that:

> *Emotional intelligence is a way of recognising, understanding and choosing how we think, feel and act. It shapes our interactions with others and our understanding of ourselves. It defines how and what we learn; it allows us to set priorities; it determines the majority of our daily actions. Research suggests it is responsible for as much as 80% of the success in our lives.*

The CAMHS Framework

Multi-agency working can be demonstrated within the CAMHS Tier Framework and within the I-Thrive model of support. Within Tier 1 every person who works with a child or young person is classed as a Tier 1 practitioner. This is the most crowded part of the triangle and where every professional discipline is represented. As you rise up the tiers, the number of practitioners reduces as specialists are identified. It is therefore imperative that this level works efficiently and together. If this level of working is right, the impact on the child/young person and their family is significant.

- The first job is to get the right people sitting around the table, at a time and location which suits all. Pursue this with a passion because this could be the crux of your solution.

- Value each other's contribution, listen with intent and accept from the start that you may not agree with each other's views and conclusions.

- Be brave to follow a colleague's lead – their idea may be best even if it makes you feel uncomfortable.

- Don't ever say '*I told you so*' and never take over another person's role because you think you can do it better.

- Be prepared to compromise.

- Go back to basics and learn about the role of your colleague – this is not to make you an expert but to enhance your understanding of how their profession works. The multi-agency mental health team I helped to create and lead developed a mental health training programme that helped many colleagues to have an understanding of mental health and how they can contribute to the professional conversation and support the assessment process.

- You may be the general in your agency but be prepared to be a foot soldier – you learn so much more in this position, recognising the role of your colleagues and the constraints they have to work within to do their job.

- Accept success and learn from your experience.

- Accept failure and learn from your mistakes.

Support for young people

We know from the many facts and figures that we are presented with on a daily basis that our young people need support.

Projections by the World Health Organization (WHO, 2011) indicate that by 2030 depression will become the most prevalent cause of ill health worldwide.

Teachers are doers; they like to get things done. Whether this is down to the fact that our days are determined by bells and movement I would not like to say, but most teachers like to feel they can go home having completed the tasks they have set themselves for the day. Once we get a backlog it can be an unsurmountable hill to climb to get back on top. We also work to the end of the day, when the pupils who have come to us and shared a range of problems have gone home. Sometimes those problems need urgent attention and a response before the pupil leaves the school. I have learnt that colleagues from other agencies do not always share my sense of urgency. That is not because I enter panic mode; it is because I know as soon as that pupil leaves my building they are potentially at risk. I have to feel that I have attempted to put in a wrap-around package of care that will help the pupil feel safe.

One of the most difficult things to navigate are the thresholds that different services put in place before they will get involved and, of course, the inevitable waiting lists that follow. This was one of the reasons that I established possibly one of the first school-based multi-agency mental health teams in the country. The challenges we faced when we embarked on that journey are discussed later in the chapter.

There are many definitions and ideas about what multi-agency is. Since the terrible death of Victoria Climbié and the subsequent serious case review, one of the main criticisms was that professionals did not speak to each other and unfortunately this criticism has been heard many times since. How sad that mistakes of the past are still impacting on our most vulnerable children and young people 20 years later. We are still seeing them die through the behaviours of the people who should be taking the best care of them, with agencies missing the signs of abuse and neglect.

What does the term 'multi-agency' mean to you?

If you searched the definition of multi-agency working you would find a plethora of answers, but I feel you have to decide which you best identify with, and which reflects your own ethos and approach.

In Rita Cheminais' book *Effective Multi-Agency Partnerships* there are two quotes I particularly like.

> *Agencies working together within a single, often new, organisational structure.*
> (Cheminais, 2009, p 24)

> *Members of different agencies work together jointly, sharing aims, information, tasks and responsibilities.*
> (Cheminais, 2009, p 20)

Here are further two statements from *Working Together to Safeguard Children*.

> *Protecting children from abuse, neglect and exploitation requires multi-agency join up and cooperation at all levels.*
>
> (HM Government, 2023, p 23)

> *Practitioners learn together by drawing on the best available evidence from their individual fields and sharing their diverse perspectives during regular shared reflection on a child's development, experiences and outcomes.*
>
> (HM Government, 2023, p 18)

REFLECTIVE TASK

- Which statement above aligns most with your way of working?
- Has your school got its own definition and where is the emphasis?

Why do we need to adopt multi-agency approaches?

One of the first questions you have to ask is what is the need for multi-agency working? I have come up with a basic list.

- There are a range of agencies and provisions working independently and not 'talking' to each other.
- We need to re-engage with the most vulnerable young people in our communities.
- A multi-agency rationale demands we move away from fragmentation.
- We need to understand the symptoms and causes of the problems.
- We need to skill up our Tier 1 and 2 workforce and referral procedures.

More often than not, groups are ignorant of each other's focus and priorities. While there are lots of agencies working together, they are not joined, which is a waste of time and resources. However, these agencies can tell a different story which is relevant to creating the bigger picture.

REFLECTIVE TASK

- What does the term 'multi-agency working' actually mean to you?
- Look at the list below and identify what multi-agency actually looks like in your school:
  - multi-agency meeting;
  - joined-up working;

→

- multi-agency working;
- integrated approach;
- partnership working;
- joint working;
- inter-agency working;
- multi-professional working;
- intra- and inter-organisational communication;
- multi-agency partnerships.

Who is in your school's multi-agency team?

There are many professionals and volunteers who work within the school environment, each providing specific support to the children and young people and hopefully to their parents and carers and to you as their colleague. This list may change dependent upon your school and age range. However, I feel it is helpful to look at who can help you within your school to effectively support both the academic and emotional well-being of your pupils.

REFLECTIVE TASK

- Using the following list, identify the key workers within your school and the role they play to support pupils.
- Once you have identified whether the staff have the relevant skills and competencies and where additional support is needed, fill in the chart in Table 7.1 and identify using your own self-assessment questions whether they need to be improved. If so, how or who could fill these in? Identify their key purpose.
  - Social worker.
  - School nurse.
  - Psychologist.
  - Mental health support worker.
  - Educational psychologist.
  - Drug and alcohol worker.
  - Counsellor.

- Speech and language therapist.
- Community police worker.
- Looked after children lead.
- Youth offending team.
- Any other workers you already have access to.

Table 7.1 Who are our multi-agency partners?

Key worker	Self-assessment questions	What is currently in place and the impact it is having	Rating (red–amber–green)	Actions and next steps to embed within the school

REFLECTIVE TASK

- Read the following story to the group of staff you are bringing together to look at your multi-agency approach. You could do the activity alone if you prefer.

The journey

- You are going on a journey. You can close your eyes; use your imagination/ feelings. At any time, you can decide when you get off the bus or stop the journey.
- Imagine you have to go somewhere you have not been before. You have the bus number and where you need to get off.

→

- — It's late at night.
- — The bus stops and you make your first steps on your journey.
- — You pay the bus driver or conductor and there are only two other people on the bus. You sit down and the journey begins.
- — The bus stops and the other two passengers get off.
- — The bus moves off and you are on your own. The bus reaches your designated stop and you get off.
- — The bus drives away.
- — The houses on the street have no lights on and the street lighting is very poor.
- — You begin to walk down the street and you are aware of footsteps behind you; you quicken up and so do the footsteps.
- — You cross the road and the footsteps cross with you.
- — You look around and notice that the footsteps belong to a man.
- — You speed up and then you feel a tap on your shoulder.
- — At what point of the journey did you feel it was time to get off the bus?
- — What would help you get on the bus in the first place? Friends, experience?

- What have you learnt by reading this story?
- Do you see any potential barriers which you may face when trying to build your multi-agency team?

Sometimes you forget how daunting it can be to set up and work in a different way, with professionals who have come from a different baseline. This is a journey I felt I made when first being asked to set up a multi-agency team. I was filled with excitement and trepidation at the same time. On reflection I may never have got on the bus.

CASE STUDY

In 2004, I was asked to set up a multi-agency mental health team. This consisted of two mental health practitioners, two family support workers and two secondary teachers. I was very excited to start this journey. Over the past 20 years, the service has developed with staff having the opportunity to improve their skillset. The team now consists of two mental health practitioners, one dramatherapist, one teacher and a co-ordinator. Their roles were to work in the secondary schools and their impact within the local authority has been outstanding. They were the interface between CAMHS and the schools, enabling early identification, assessments and interventions to take place. They have helped develop school-based services, working with the schools, providing training and developing a mental health training course that was nationally recognised. Three of the founding members still work within the team and they shared their views on what their role has been and both the advantages and disadvantages of this team.

1. *A good multi-agency mental health team will be respectful of the expertise, experience, training, codes of conduct and alternative perspectives of the different professionals making up the team. The team will be clear about routine and regular clinical, managerial and peer supervision and safeguarding. The multi-agency aspect of the team will enable all the practitioners to be aware of the systems in school and be mindful of the considerable knowledge, systems etc in the school or settings they are working within.*

2. *The team can provide the expertise not available within the school setting from mental health professionals to ensure pupils can be seen where this will cause as little disruption to their usual routines, particularly around being in school. A team like this can provide the schools with the additionality of working alongside health professionals, for example the school nurse, in identifying and then providing early intervention in familiar settings for the pupils and working closely with them to continue the work most appropriate to the needs of the pupils. Long-term relationships with these schools can help to break down the barriers between health and education, demystify CAMHS, mental health assessments and ultimately support staff's confidence in mental health and well-being interventions. Linking the schools, families and mental health workers together means you are continually learning from others and ensures a joined-up holistic approach that most benefits the young person.*

3. *The difficulties of working in this sort of team are minimal but can be around loss of confidence in your professional identity, entitlement to specific training that may only be available to those registered in a certain profession and differential access to systems. As a mental health team sitting within education, it is imperative that continued professional development from the CAMHS service is provided.*

Establishing multi-agency working

Creating the team was hard. I cannot use any other word. My deputy and I had to use every ounce of energy to get colleagues from different agencies to work together and to somehow fuse their own professional disciplines. There was no book we did not read and every Monday morning after reading yet another text from Daniel Goleman, such as *Emotional Intelligence*, *Working with Emotional Intelligence* and *The New Leaders*, plus many others, we would greet every Monday morning with the inspiration to try another approach. Sometimes it worked, sometimes it didn't but eventually we found the solution.

To Margaret, I will be eternally grateful; she kept me grounded, but I am also grateful to several members of the team who got what we were trying to do. Those that didn't were moved on, not by me but by their service leads who recognised they did not have the right approach.

What follows next is some step-by-step guidance on how to establish multi-agency working in your school. This is practical advice and can and should be tweaked to suit your community.

Practical strategies for multi-agency working

- Work with who you are, not where you think you should be.
- Develop confidence.
- Create meaningful relationships.
- Listen with action.

The way forward is to:

- identify your team and create your own baseline – it will be different for each of you;
- have clear directions and expectations – empower your staff to have responsibility to make decisions;
- establish who you will be linking with – invest time in creating relationships which have a common understanding. I have always found a cup of tea and some biscuits, especially chocolate ones, helps immensely;
- don't just listen – plan what needs to be done;
- acknowledge your anxieties – use them as a learning point – if you have these anxieties, the chances are so does everyone else.

When looking at multi-agency work, each setting has to share where they get their information from. Generally, this information is gleaned from agencies involved with the child or young person, from the young person themselves and from their parents or carers. You need to decide what this information is telling you and how you collaboratively analyse this information. You can then adapt and be reactive or pro-active. If you act reactively, you refer immediately to specialist services and, as I would say, pass your monkey to another professional, or you could be reactive and implement interventions with professionals helping you in that process.

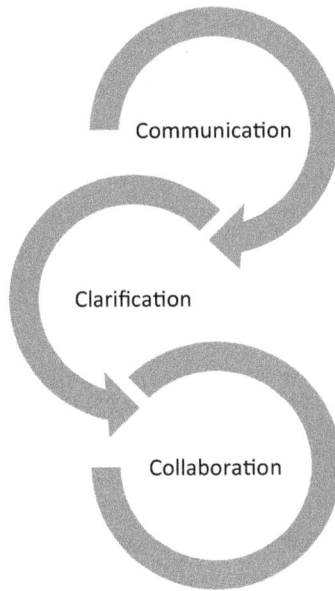

Figure 7.1 *The basic principles of effective multi-agency working*

The diagram above shows how multi-agency working is improved if we implement effective communication, clarification and collaborative principles in implementing change.

Communication

Communication can be categorised into three basic groups:

1. verbal communication, where you *listen* to a person and understand what they are saying;

2. written communication, where you read what the person is meaning and saying;

3. non-verbal communication, where you observe a person and infer what they are saying. This form of communication is very difficult to interpret in the world of Zoom and Teams so try and get people to sit around a table.

Clarification

Clarification is about what you hope to achieve and to make the problem look less confusing and easier to understand. Emails and texts are prime examples of how we can misinterpret what is being said, and clarification of the sender's meaning can often start with a negative mindset.

Collaboration

Collaboration is when the theory becomes practice. This is where the individuals come together for a common purpose – to make things better for the child/young person, their families and the school community.

Barriers to multi-agency working

There will be initial barriers to multi-agency/multi-disciplinary working which need to be recognised.

- Different professional and disciplinary traditions and cultures. We all need to acknowledge where we come from and that you won't always sing from the same hymn sheet. Our professional status is very important to each and every one of us. We should never dismiss our professional status and I don't think it should be passed to one side in the process.

- The IT systems from different services do not work together. IT systems cannot be shared and they will very rarely talk to each other – that's the machine and human being. This makes it very difficult when you have a CAMHS team and a local authority team working together. Duplicate systems often have to be established or staff have to work across sites. Doing double paperwork is nonsense and eats up precious time which could be spent with a client.

- Supervision is essential for safeguarding of members of the team and there should be clarity around what is supervision and what is mentoring, which can easily be confused.

- There is often a lack of shared perspectives and understanding. We must work with each other to understand each other's point of view and that there are different professional priorities. Accept these differences and build them into your business plan.

- Within different professions, in different authorities, there will be organisational structures and working practices which seem hard to understand. Look at these structures and practices with an open mind and be prepared to change the way you work and come out of your comfort zone. Sitting within different directorates and places of work is just geography; it's not about losing your professional identity.

- Confidentiality of the information you have received is important. You must always respect that confidentiality, but don't use it against your colleagues. If you are working in a team, there has to be a clear agreement that all the information can be shared. No one has the right to put their colleague in a situation where their working with a pupil has left them vulnerable and unsafe. This completely undermines multi-agency working, but it does happen. I did hear on several occasions, '*I cannot share that information with you as only health/social care colleagues can be told*'. My question would always be '*Why?*'

- Relationships between the professional and 'service user' need to be clear. When working with pupils and their families it can be so easy to become embroiled in their problem, but you must always keep a safe distance. Know your role, who's who and what you can realistically deliver. You are not their friend!

- The team will experience the same pressures as those on the wider public where we could ignore children's rights, have denial of the abuse shared and be reluctant to intervene. We experience the same pressures as everyone else even though we sit within a team.

Challenges for the leadership team

Challenges can come to everyone; there is no caveat that states that anyone in the team is immune to the challenges they face.

- How diverse is the organisation you are leading? Where does the potential multi-agency team come from – and what professional bodies and standards do they have to work towards? You are not being asked to know everything but to understand those needs.

- What is the expectation of the leadership team? Do they expect the leader to know it all or to be seen as part of that development team, wanting to be supported and guided through the planning with the colleagues sitting with them?

- What is the expectation of staff who they appoint to the team and what are the expectations of the team? Are they ready to trip you up or catch you when you fall?

- What are the expectations of the local authority children services, health and social care departments and where will this team sit within the school and directorate – whom do you report to?

- What are the anxieties you have around multi-agency working? There is often a lot of anxiety around being deskilled and working outside your comfort zone. Questions asked include, '*How will I maintain my professional standards?*'

Once the team are established, there are potential challenges for the staff directly and indirectly involved and these must be considered for the benefit of everyone.

- Who has the final say in the decision making or will it be a whole team decision? There can be conflict around professional decisions but we must accept that sometimes we must follow, not lead, and learn from the process. If it does not work, we do not apportion blame but look at what went well and what we could do better.

- There is different legislation for each professional group. Unfortunately, no one in the echelons of government has sat down to try and knit these together. Where it does exist, it is as is often the case open for interpretation.

- Acknowledge the three P's – Policies, Procedures and Practice. Make sure these are in place before you start and agreed by all. This will bring about empowerment and joint ownership, which will lead to success. This should not be an afterthought, an add-on.

- The team should have confidence in the ability of colleagues and know they are all working supportively.

- You need to understand each other's roles and to know what you are all doing. Remember that people from different agencies will see the problems and issues from a different perspective – this does not make it wrong if it does not align with your views; it means an informed and detailed discussion needs to take place with aspects of everyone's feeling included in the way forward.

Finally, I believe there are four principal motivators for people to come to work:

1. respect;
2. responsibility;
3. reward;
4. recognition.

REFLECTIVE TASK

- How do you ensure the four principles of respect, responsibility, reward and recognition happen within your school?

If we take the figure that one in four children will have some level of mental health need then you could believe that 25 per cent of pupils need a referral.

So how do you decide who needs referring to more specialist services – is it the pupil whom you like or is it the learner who really does need the help? The job is to look at the whole so that no one falls through the net.

REFLECTIVE TASK

- Using the model in Figure 7.2, how do you first implement a whole school approach and then prioritise your referrals for additional support?

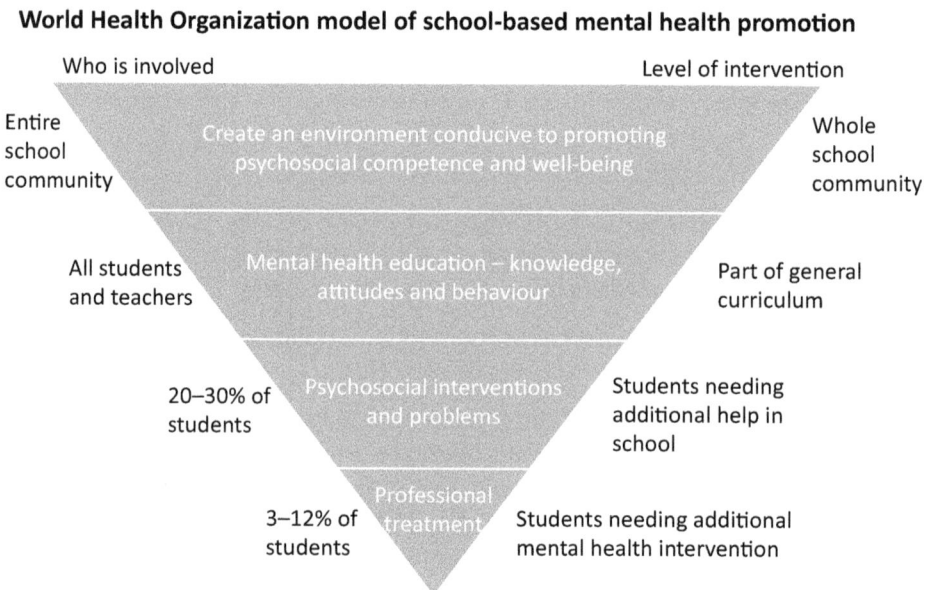

World Health Organization model of school-based mental health promotion

Who is involved	Level of intervention
Entire school community	Create an environment conducive to promoting psychosocial competence and well-being	Whole school community

Who is involved	Level of intervention
Entire school community	Create an environment conducive to promoting psychosocial competence and well-being	Whole school community
All students and teachers	Mental health education – knowledge, attitudes and behaviour	Part of general curriculum
20–30% of students	Psychosocial interventions and problems	Students needing additional help in school
3–12% of students	Professional treatment	Students needing additional mental health intervention

Figure 7.2 *Developing a multi-agency mental health team within your school (Wyn et al, 2000)*

> *Education is not just about attainment: it should also enable children to develop their personalities, talents and abilities, to build resilience, self-esteem and to live a full and satisfying life.*
>
> (The Marmot Review, 2010, p 104)

I like this quote because this is what education should be about. Academic learning is very important but if a child or young person does not have the emotional skills and well-being to function in society, then their exams will not be enough. Schools who work in a multi-agency way are not following a new way of working. Each child and young person's emotional well-being is quite simply the responsibility of everyone, and everyone's contributions need to be recognised when we have to untangle complex problems.

When I was training school staff on mental health, I would often get a new sheet of A4 paper and explain how lovely it was – no creases, nothing written on it, and align it with a newborn baby. I would then screw up the paper rather aggressively and then try to make that sheet of paper perfect again. It was impossible. But we are all that 'crumpled' piece of paper with our life experiences etched into every crease. It reminded us all that whatever we do, our children have one chance. It's our duty to ensure they access the right support at the right time and that a referral is made with good information.

CAMHS services across the country have gone through significant changes and again each area, due to financial and geographical division, can provide different services even though they sit within a standard of principles around delivery times and provision. I have attempted to provide a quick reference below. The previous chapters contain the most up-to-date guidance for education, CAMHS/health services and social care.

CAMHS services feel all children and young people should:

- have the ability to develop psychologically, emotionally, intellectually, culturally and spiritually;
- be safe from psychological trauma and abuse;
- have their wishes and feelings taken into consideration;
- have equal and timely access to appropriate, high-quality, mental health services.

This vision will be realised by:

- mental health promotion at all levels of service;
- inter-agency working with joint protocols and policies;
- services provided at suitable locations and convenient times;
- consideration of socio-economic and familial factors on some young people;
- early intervention;
- young people being involved and consulted in decision making.

They need to develop a capable and competent team which demonstrates a competence-based skill mix, based on analysis of the evidence of effective practice, which will be based on three levels in keeping with Child Outcomes Research Consortium (CORC) (Wolpert et al, 2016) principles:

1. research-based evidence;
2. values-based evidence;
3. practice-based evidence.

In 2017, the government published a consultation called *Transforming Children and Young People's Mental Health Provision: A Green Paper* (DoH and DfE, 2017, p 7). Within this there were three core proposals.

1. *New mental health support teams (MHSTs) in 20–25 per cent of the country by 2023/24 that provide support and extra capacity for early intervention and help for mild to moderate mental health issues.*
2. *Training for senior mental health leads to implement an effective whole school or college approach to mental health and wellbeing in schools and colleges.*
3. *Pilots of four-week waiting time for children and young people's mental health services.*

The policy objectives are to:

*   *promote good mental health and wellbeing amongst all CYP through whole school approaches and effective joint working;*
*   *increase access to appropriate support for CYP with mild to moderate mental health conditions in England; and*
*   *improve access to and reduce waiting times for specialist NHS CYPMHS for those who need it.*

The intended outcome is to improve mental health and well-being among children and young people, generating benefits for the children and young people, their families and wider society.

To respond in part to the above, schools need to:

*   produce an analysis of skills gaps to inform their support and training needs;
*   produce a development plan for the mental health implementation which feeds into their school development plan, the primary care trust (PCT) Self-Assessment, the Children's Directorate within the local authority and any other local initiatives;
*   audit the skill mix of the team they currently have and aspire to have in place.

However, to achieve some of the above we need to have a shared identity, purpose and vision. If we do not do this, we will once again end up with a fragmented workforce with the following characteristics:

*   workforce identity often based on occupational groups;
*   presence of these separate identities and lack of a coherent vision impedes change.

Instead, what we really want is a reformed workforce who have:

- shared identity and a shared vision of better services for children;
- organisational changes led and managed within a strong sense of purpose;
- an understanding that working in partnership is part of the day job.

Some of the things schools need to do to promote emotional and mental well-being within their school can be easily implemented but need clear thought and planning.

These are some considerations.

- Leadership and management. Who will lead on the team's development? I would suggest this is a member of the senior leadership team who can influence the school workforce and have the authority to manage these changes.
- Staff development and well-being. All staff need to feel that they are being listened to. I firmly believe that the emotional well-being and needs of the staff have to be in place for them to see the benefits of cascading this to the children and young people in the school.
- Ethos and environment. Look at your environment and the story it tells. It does not need to be the most up-to-date building but a welcoming environment should be seen within the ethos and the way the classrooms and general areas are seen.
- Curriculum and teaching. What is the teaching and learning message? Are the staff encouraged to teach with empathy and understanding? Is it just about results?
- Student voice. Never put a provision in place without asking the pupils what they want. An adult's perception may not correlate with what is actually needed.
- Identifying need and monitoring impact. Once the need has been identified, how will you monitor impact? Will it be improved attendance, reduction in behaviour incidents? Or academic progress?

Multi-agency working implemented effectively can have a significant impact on your school, including the academic progress all the pupils can make. If a child feels safe, they will learn and their voices need to be heard, supported and listened to. We need to learn to listen with intent, notice the unsaid feelings and emotions and treat them with empathy.

Final thought

Glasby and Peck (2012, p 7) in their paper 'We have to stop meeting like this: the governance of inter-agency partnerships', stated that '*To elaborate, partnership working should always be a means to an end (of better services and hence of better outcomes) for service users and their families. The issues debated should never become an end in themselves*'.

KEY POINTS

- There is no 'I' in team.
- This is not 'rocket science' – multi-agency working is about connection and human relationships.
- Understand what the term 'multi-agency' means.
- How does your school promote multi-agency working and does the current ethos promote staff well-being? This needs to be in place before staff can be asked to demonstrate empathy, understanding and support to your pupils.
- Complete a school analysis of who supports your school and what is currently missing.
- Build a skills analysis of your staff and identify which skills are missing. Ensure that there is in place a comprehensive CPD programme for staff to understand the purpose and values of multi-agency working.
- What are the main difficulties of pupils in your school? What specific help do they need to be positive learners and, equally important, how do you support their emotional well-being?
- Make sure that your multi-agency team feel part of the school and are included in your decision making – they should not be seen as a visitor but part of the school staff and work within your school ethos.
- Be prepared to make mistakes but learn from them.

Further reading

Dogra, N, Parkin, A, Gale, F and Frake, C (2009) *A Multi-disciplinary Handbook of Child and Adolescent Mental Health for Frontline Professionals*. London: Jessica Kingsley Publishers.

Institute of Health Equity (2020) *Health Equity in England: The Marmot Review 10 Years On*. [online] Available at: www.health.org.uk/publications/reports/the-marmot-review-10-years-on (accessed 9 January 2024).

Kotter, J (2006) *Our Iceberg Is Melting: Changing and Succeeding under Any Conditions*. London: Pan Macmillan Ltd.

Long, R and Fogell, J (1999) *Supporting Pupils with Emotional Difficulties: Creating a Caring Environment for All*. London: David Fulton Publishers.

Walker, G (2018) *Working Together for Children: A Critical Introduction to Multi-Agency Working*. 2nd ed. London: Bloomsbury.

References

Cheminais, R (2009) *Effective Multi-Agency Partnerships. Putting Every Child Matters into Practice*. London: Sage Publications Ltd.

Department for Education (DfE) (2003) *Every Child Matters*. [online] Available at: www.gov.uk/government/publications/every-child-matters (accessed 9 January 2024).

Department for Education (DfE) (2008) *Back on Track: A Strategy for Modernising Alternative Provision for Young People*. White Paper. [online] Available at: https://assets.publishing.service.gov.uk/media/5a7de67be5274a2e8ab448b3/Back_on_Track.pdf (accessed 9 January 2024).

Department for Education (DfE) (2012) *Multi Agency Working*.

Department for Education (DfE) (2022) *Transforming Children and Young People's Mental Health Implementation Programme*. [online] Available at: www.gov.uk/government/publications/transforming-children-and-young-peoples-mental-health-provision (accessed 9 January 2024).

Department for Education (DfE) (2023) *Special Educational Needs and Disabilities (SEND) and Alternative Provision (AP) Improvement Plan: Right Support, Right Place, Right Time*. [online] Available at: www.gov.uk/government/publications/send-and-alternative-provision-improvement-plan (accessed 9 January 2024).

Department of Health (DoH) and Department for Education (DfE) (2017) *Transforming Children and Young People's Mental Health Provision: A Green Paper*. [online] Available at: https://assets.publishing.service.gov.uk/media/5a823518e5274a2e87dc1b56/Transforming_children_and_young_people_s_mental_health_provision.pdf (accessed 9 January 2024).

Freedman, J M (1998) *Handle with Care: The Emotional Intelligence Activity Book*. Freedom, CA: Six Seconds.

Glasby, J and Peck, E (2012) *We Have to Stop Meeting Like This: The Governance of Inter-Agency Partnerships*. Policy Paper. Birmingham: University of Birmingham.

Goleman, D (1996) *Emotional Intelligence: Why It Can Matter More than IQ*. London: Bloomsbury.

Goleman, D (1999) *Working with Emotional Intelligence*. London: Bloomsbury.

Goleman, D, Boyatzis, R and McKee, A (2002) *The New Leaders: Transforming the Art of Leadership into the Science of Results*. London: Time Warner Paperbacks.

HM Government (2023) Working Together to Safeguard Children 2023. [online] Available at: https://assets.publishing.service.gov.uk/media/65cb4349a7ded0000c79e4e1/Working_together_to_safeguard_children_2023_-_statutory_guidance.pdf (accessed 1 March 2024).

The Marmot Review (2010) *Fair Society, Healthy Lives: The Marmot Review*. [online] Available at: www.parliament.uk/globalassets/documents/fair-society-healthy-lives-full-report.pdf (accessed 9 January 2024).

Wolpert, M, Jacob, J, Napoleone, E, Whale, A, Calderon, A and Edbrooke-Childs, J (2016) Child- and Parent-reported Outcomes and Experience from *Child and Young People's Mental Health Services 2011–2015*. London: CAMHS Press.

World Health Organization (WHO) (2011) Global Burden of Mental Disorders and the Need for a Comprehensive, Coordinated Response From Health and Social Sectors at the Country Level: Report by the Secretariat. [online] Available at: https://apps.who.int/gb/ebwha/pdf_files/EB130/B130_9-en.pdf (accessed 21 February 2024).

Wyn, J, Cahill, H, Holdsworth, R, Rowling, L and Carson, S (2000) MindMatters, a Whole-school Approach Promoting Mental Health and Wellbeing. *Australian and New Zealand Journal of Psychiatry*, 34(4): 594–601.

8   And along came Alice ...

During a phone call at my third inspection with the lead inspector she called me 'odd'. I thought how rude was that? When she came into my office the next day, she said, '*I think I offended you yesterday but what I meant was that most headteachers of PRUs leave after six or seven years as they are burnt out, but you have been here ten years*'. I often wonder what she would say if she knew I had stayed for 25 years! Maybe if she reads this chapter, she may understand why.

Throughout my career, I have always worked with those pupils who appeared reticent to learn. I could write pages on those pupils and I can recall three memorable occasions from my early years I would like to share.

1.   In my first teaching job, I was given a group of 15 Year 10 pupils who no one knew what to do with. They asked me to teach them ballroom dancing as I had said on my application that I had done ballroom dancing in my youth. Imagine, if you can, coercing a group of loud, unco-operative pupils to dance together and learn the barn dance and waltz.

2.   My headteacher walked into one of my lessons and was astounded that two of the noisiest Year 7 pupils were sitting working. She asked me to step outside of the classroom and asked what I had done. I had to admit that I had made very chewy bonfire toffee and that I had given a piece to each pupil in the class so they would do the work I had set. She asked that a jar of toffee was made for her and the story goes that pupils were offered a piece before she started to speak to them about their behaviour as they could not respond!

3.   When I worked in one of the most deprived areas of Greater Manchester, I took a group of pupils to the Ideal Home Exhibition at Earl's Court. None of those pupils left my side – tough in their own environment, lost in the bigger world – which highlighted to me the importance of the attachment they had to their environment and the trust they had in me.

I realised I had an affinity with those pupils whose SEMH needs I could respond to and support.

Introduction

Pupil 1:	*Miss, have you heard of this woman called Mrs Cahill?*
Deputy headteacher:	*Yes, I have, why?*
Pupil 1:	*K never stops talking about her, she sounds amazing.*
Pupil 2 (K):	*She is amazing but you don't mess with her!*

I have been fortunate to support a few thousand pupils during my time as a headteacher of a PRU. They all left a footprint on my professional journey and I learnt as much from them as they learnt from me: what it means to care. The title of this chapter reflects those pupils who have been under my care. I realised that you cannot work with these pupils and stay detached. Their life experiences touched my soul and while not thinking I could solve all their problems, I knew I had to help them find their own solutions. On admission, when I asked pupils what they wanted from me, they would say they just wanted to be 'normal', whatever that might be, but basically they wanted to 'fit in' and be like their friends in school. In 1994, Vera Fahlberg wrote:

> *Throughout spring we see sprouts emerging from the ground. Stalks spring up, they leaf, they bud and finally they blossom. Some show themselves earlier and grow faster than others. Some lag behind the crowd. But no matter what the timing, the progression from stalk to leaf to bud to blossom is the same.*
>
> *Careful inspection of the blossoms reveal that although they are more similar than different, each is unique.*

For most of my pupils it just took them a bit longer to grow and with that bit of extra support, they all finished their time in school in line with their peers.

This chapter is about why I became a teacher, my experiences of SEMH and why if you embrace that pupil who is just a little different, your working day can be greatly enriched.

There will always be an 'Alice' in your class.

My belief

My ethos of education has never floundered in 42 years. I believe that all children are born good but like everyone, they can make poor choices. But we all deserve a second chance in life and I hope I have helped my pupils reflect on some of those choices and that they felt better placed to move into their next phase of education.

In 1990, at Madison Park High School, Roxbury, Nelson Mandela said that:

> *Education is the most powerful weapon we can use to change the world. Changing the world requires first changing minds – and since education is so deeply linked to persuasion, it is no surprise that it is such an effective tool.*

I knew that all my pupils were 'emotionally' armed to move forward in their lives. They had all worked hard to address their difficulties and were rightfully proud of the progress they had made. I would tell them that the best advice I could give them was to remember education does not only take place in stuffy classrooms. It can happen anywhere, anytime to anyone, but whatever they did, they must also spend some time working on whatever they were passionate about in life. I have been lucky to do this and why should I not wish the same for my pupils?

Sometimes the experiences we have during early adolescence stay with us forever and they contribute to the person we become. It is said that by the age of two all the building blocks of our brain development are in place but I think it is only when you hit your mid-teens that we truly begin to understand the power of emotions and the impact they have on our daily routines. My pupils had a range of experiences, some positive, some negative, and only they could decide which ones should stay with them and which ones they should get rid of. One of the quotations I would share with my pupils was by Carlos Castaneda (1998, p 16):

> Look at every path closely and deliberately.
>
> Try it as many times as you think necessary. Then ask yourself one question... does this path have a heart?
>
> If it does, the path is good; if it doesn't it is of no use.

At the end of each academic year and especially when my Year 11 pupils were leaving, we had an end-of-year celebration. It was really important to talk about my pupils in a positive way and I would often relate their journey to a story. I have used the story of the *Wizard of Oz*, where my director aligned me to the Wicked Witch of the West, not Dorothy with the magical red shoes, and the story of my 50th birthday paragliding experience and fear of falling into the sea and being eaten by sharks. I had hoped that the comments from the same director would be positive, portraying my tenacity and determination but instead he was more concerned for the sharks!

Those afternoons were not about the staff and me but about the pupils, their families and the schools they had attended. I could observe and see the tangible impact we had on these young people. I saw families mended where parents and carers and the wider family showed their pride in what they had overcome and how far they had come – families and relationships healed, positive futures planned and a sense of achievement. Earlier in the book, I discussed how many parents and carers just wanted their child to finish school and move on – if they got qualifications that would be a bonus. But my pupils did get qualifications and finished their school experience feeling positive and pleased that they had persevered. Their school experience had highlighted not only the many difficulties they had faced but also their many strengths.

It would therefore be only fitting for this chapter to be about them, my pupils, their stories and why a PRU placement had been the right decision for them alongside the school experience and attendance which continued.

CASE STUDY

Walking towards the PRU I was apprehensive. My child did not cope well in main-stream and had been out of formal education for over a year. As I walked through the door my worries and fears melted away. My child was not keen to engage at first but as the staff showed me around, I was really impressed with how calm and nurturing it was. I knew my child would succeed here. The support was shared with the whole family, not just the pupil. When we had a major tragedy in the family the headteacher called me at home and offered her support. She asked me to call in her office when I dropped my child off and she spent a lot of time listening to me, I will never forget her kindness. The support they gave my child was immeasurable. They thrived men-tally and educationally, achieving exceptional grades at GCSE. After leaving the PRU my child attended one of the top universities in the country. I cannot praise and thank the headteacher and staff enough.

Sue, parent

The untapped talents in a PRU

Quotations can be really effective at capturing and concisely communicating thoughts and ideas. They can be inspirational but more importantly quotations can help us reveal and assess the assumptions, values and beliefs that underlie the ways in which we per-ceive the world.

We are all very quick to make assumptions when we meet people. When pupils attend a PRU, many people will also make assumptions. Here are a few.

- In 2012, Michael Gove stated, '*All PRUs are not "up to snuff"*'.
- In May 2014, the Welsh commissioner was so disappointed with the PRUs in Wales that it was stated '*Pupil referral units damage children's well-being*'.
- In 2012, a study by the independent think tank Demos found that only 1 per cent of excluded children received the equivalent of five A* to C grades at GCSE level, compared with 70 per cent of pupils who remained in school (Reidy, 2012).

Would I agree with these assumptions and beliefs? Absolutely not. PRUs are not dumping grounds or sin bins. They should not be a place for pupils to grow their entrenched, often poor behaviour. Staff should be committed to putting in place structures and systems that allow pupils to flourish, which often means providing 'tough love'.

I often wished my esteemed colleagues would come and sit quietly in my unit and listen and learn first-hand what we do with such amazing young people. The only education min-ister to do this was Nadhim Zahawi, who listened to my pupils' journey, their experiences in school, at the PRU and their aspirations. On leaving he suggested that my PRU and myself should be cloned. The look of terror on my pupils' and staff's faces raised many hours of laughter.

I am always in awe when I reflect on the pupils who are about to leave me. I look at the progress they have made, their personal journeys which have not been easy by anyone's standards and where they are now. For quite a long time, many of them kept 'banging their heads' as they could not work out how it could be different for them when starting at the PRU from their experience of mainstream school. They needed to take some 'time out' to think and I know I helped them put themselves back together and learn how to move forward without being hurt.

Life is hard but it is often interspersed with moments of great happiness and joy. The trouble is we don't always recognise these moments and that brings me back to my final quotation.

This is not from anyone universally famous, but from someone who became widely known within my PRU community because of their quote we saw every day; it helped everyone to take a quiet moment of reflection and smile.

> *This is life, a wonderful gift. Accept it, embrace it.*
>
> *It starts with a new day, wake up and greet it.*
>
> (2014)

We fail if we do not send a pupil back to a mainstream or special school setting. We fail because we believe that an 'alternative setting' is the only place a pupil can thrive. But staying in a PRU or AP is not real life. Your pupils have to go back into the real world and work in their community. If they feel safe in the PRU they will stay, but I knew I needed to challenge their fears – feel the fear but do it anyway is a saying I would use. Containment does not solve the problem.

In my opinion, PRUs and APs are full of untapped talent: pupils whose strengths have not been recognised and who will begin to respond negatively to the environment they are in.

REFLECTIVE TASK

> *An educational system isn't worth a great deal if it teaches young people how to make a living but doesn't teach them how to make a life.*
>
> (Author unknown)

- For better or worse, we all cast a shadow. What kind of shadow do you think you cast and why?

- How we behave and conduct ourselves will have a massive effect on the culture of our school. What do you do to ensure that pupils develop those unseen qualities needed to survive in the outside world?

My pupils' journeys

As previously mentioned, there are so many stories I could share of my pupils' journeys through the PRU. Many have gone on to be academically very successful; I have helped my pupils become teachers, nurses, doctors, social workers and successful business people. More importantly, they have left to lead happy and successful lives and, as they asked on admission, to be just like their friends. Here are three case studies to illustrate this.

CASE STUDY 1

Previously a hard-working, high-level student who at the time struggled to fit in socially, I fell into the wrong crowd in the middle of secondary school. As a result of this I slowly became more rebellious and 'naughty'. I began to get into more and more trouble at school, pushing boundaries, arguing with teachers, skiving lessons. This behaviour didn't just stay in school. I began smoking weed and drinking, inviting my newfound group of friends to my house where we would cause trouble. As well as my behaviour my mental health started to decline, often getting anxious and upset. I was referred to CAMHS and a drug and alcohol worker and put on a protection plan. My mum was struggling to control me at this point and I was kicked out of school for an offence relating to the weed. Due to this being a month before the summer holidays I wouldn't be found another school until the next school year. This also gave more time for me to be a nuisance, often being reported missing; I ended up knowing a lot of the local police.

When it came to going back to school, I was put on an integration path to start at a PRU and slowly be integrated back into a mainstream school. I started at the PRU and was shocked at how different it was from mainstream school. The classes were so much smaller, which meant there was more time with teachers and less people to be overwhelmed by. I loved this school. The teachers went the extra mile to make sure we were learning while also being kept engaged with. I was still causing trouble in and out of school though, still being reported missing as well as being removed from my mum's care and moving to live with my dad. I was still arguing with teachers when there was something I didn't want to do but the PRU put more provisions in to try to keep me on the right track, for example realising that I sometimes worked better on my own in a separate room when I didn't have people to distract or be distracted by.

This was only a temporary placement though and I still had to go back to mainstream school. I struggled at the new school allocated and this ultimately failed as well. My first school had rescinded the exclusion and as it was my last year I returned there. I was still taking liberties though; still, I think the PRU really helped me heal the damage I had caused myself at the time. I was being destructive to try to fit in. I enjoyed it. But the PRU showed me that there were better, more positive things to bring me

→

joy such as my art and product design. I started my product design GCSE when I was at my first school and was very passionate about this. I was so grateful to the PRU for arranging for me to go to a different school after hours to enable me to finish the practical side as well as staff spending extra time with me to help me finish the writing side. The PRU put more provisions in to stop me wanting to skip lessons and I ended up passing all of my GCSEs, something I definitely wouldn't have done without them.

I went to college and completed my level 2 diploma in art, left education to go to work for two years, then decided to go back to education. I've just finished my Foundation Level 4 Diploma in art and design and have an unconditional place for September at Cardiff Metropolitan to do Maker: Artist Designer.

I thoroughly believe that had the PRU not saw something in me and encouraged me to continue with what I enjoyed I wouldn't be doing what I am now. I probably wouldn't have had the grades to go back to education and I wouldn't believe in myself as much as I do.

Lizzie, pupil

CASE STUDY 2

'Puberty and the inability to self-regulate is hard' would be the understatement of the century. My dad died very suddenly when I was just eight and my mum was left alone with zero emotional or financial support; money was incredibly tight and we struggled to have the basics of food, clothing and heating. My mum worked but she struggled with addiction and substance abuse.

I am sharing all this to give you an insight as to why secondary school was so hard. I was bullied relentlessly. Nobody wants to be a friend to the girl whose smile doesn't quite reach her eyes, wearing too big cast-off clothes and a scruffy uniform that reeks of smoke even though she doesn't smoke. After two years of torture having attended two mainstream schools, I ended up in quite a bad fight being burnt with a lighter and had my clipper card stolen. I was school refusing, frightened to tell my mum the whole shame-inducing, ugly truth.

My emotional state at that time was possibly as bad as it had ever been other than when my father passed away without any warning. I was in a constant state of fear, shame and terror. Of course, the law states I had to go to school, so I ended up in a PRU. My mum's health was deteriorating and life at home was hard with my brother acting out. Everything just seemed like a battle. I remember starting at the PRU feeling scared, guarded, vulnerable and very angry. Everything and everyone were not only unhelpful but untrustworthy. My resilience was at an all-time low, but the one thing I was determined to do was to not let my wall down and I built my wall so high, not one soul was peeking over the top.

When I started at the PRU and to my astonishment and annoyance, most of the staff at the PRU did care despite me continuing to verbally abuse not only the staff but fellow students; I made it my mission to disrupt lessons. I would try anything to push staff away, even drinking and smoking on a school trip, but the staff still stayed by my side. In particular, the no-nonsense headteacher would not give up on me. I'd be quite resourceful and imaginative in my ways of unleashing havoc on the centre, the students and staff but it was myself that was just as hurt or affected by it. I always was one for cutting off my own nose to spite my face. I thought if I was relentless, they'll give up and see what I see and they'll come to feel about me the same way that I see myself, a nothing, a nobody, undeserving of basic things. Annoyingly they didn't. The staff could see something in me, even if I couldn't. I would give the impression of disinterest in most lessons, but especially in English I was lucky enough to have two excellent teachers who drew me into the world of Macbeth and Frankenstein's monster. I even enjoyed science, the teacher worked absolute miracles to keep me in her classroom and even occasionally produce work. I absolutely loved PSHE and drama with a teacher that went on to become my friend. I tried on numerous occasions to disrupt her lessons, but she would have the whole class leave the room, quite rightly, and asked me to self-reflect. I slowly let down my guard and made progress not just academically, but also socially and emotionally.

Life decided to knock me back again when my mother was diagnosed with lung and liver cancer. It was terminal; she had months to live. Life was unbearable. I was terrified. When I did manage to get into school, the head went above and beyond what any sane person would do for me. I was unbearable to be around, but she was there even in moments when I didn't want her to be. I was ashamed of myself, my house, my life, my brother, but never my mum and the head personally drove me to and from the hospital, as I had no bus fare to get to the hospital and see my mum otherwise. She tried her very best to get me into school, waiving her usual policies on school uniform and lateness. Not that I cared about any of that. At the time I was drowning and there was no shore in sight. My mum died on New Year's Eve, 2005 and I felt as if my world shattered into a million pieces. But the PRU provided me a 'safe base' for the last six months of my education.

Fast forward 17 years, I have a partner of 14 years and we have two beautiful daughters; we both work and we are good parents. I honestly believe without the kindness, consistency, expertise, decency and compassion I was lucky enough to encounter through the relationships made at the PRU, whether or not I thought I wanted or needed them, that I would not be the person I am today. I might not have even made it to the ripe old age of 33. I will also give myself some credit because I've been through some bad times but I'm an alright person. I am kind, I love my family, friends, colleagues and students at the schools. I've worked in the mainstream school and now in the PRU. Teenage Alice would be cringing.

Alice, pupil

CASE STUDY 3

It's difficult to describe what the PRU felt like to me because the truth is that, unlike every school I had attended prior, it just felt 'normal'. Before arriving at the PRU I constantly felt like I had to be looking over my shoulder, that there was a target on my back for bullying that was always at the front of my mind. The PRU, despite being far from a typical school, allowed me to feel at home so I could focus on progressing both academically and as a person.

Upon moving onwards to college and university, it was possible to find people who shared my passions and use that to form connections and feel like part of a community. What makes the experience of the PRU truly incredible to me is that the community was so much more diverse, being made up of people from many different backgrounds and interests who just shared a difficult experience in their schools. For the staff to be able to take such a varied group of teenagers and create a tight-knit community that allowed us to feel safe is an achievement that I find it difficult to comprehend, and yet I was able to live through it and benefit from it.

I will forever be thankful for the dedication and support given to me by the entire PRU team. They helped guide me through some of the darkest moments of my life and gave me confidence to move forward to heights I could never have imagined.

Olivia, pupil

Final thought

On admission, I would tell my pupils and parents/carers that if I saw them outside of the PRU I would not acknowledge them first. I was not being rude, but for some, their time in the PRU was personal and by me not drawing attention to myself, their wider family and friends would not know they were not attending their mainstream school.

A headteacher (me) walks into a pub in another city with her son.

A woman walks towards her and the headteacher whispers to her son, there is one of my ex-pupils.

The woman seeing the headteacher freezes, turns around and retraces her steps.

The woman returns and comes towards the headteacher smiling with her arms open and gives her a hug.

Throughout the meal the woman hovers, checking that they are still eating.

As they finish the meal she comes across and asks if everything was okay and if she could have a word.

She bends down at the side of the table, takes the headteacher's hands and quietly thanks her for everything. Words are said and tears shed.

She asked if I would like a cup of tea – something she said she still enjoyed as I always offered a cup of tea to everyone to relax.

I had not seen this pupil for over 20 years, but I remember her journey and it was so good to know that she had survived her demons and was living a happy life.

We are never aware of how long the impact we have on our pupils will last – but it's usually a lifetime.

KEY POINTS

- There is no 'I' in team – I would never have achieved so much without the team I had.

- This is not 'rocket science' – it's about human relationships, believing in the people you meet and helping them achieve their potential.

- My mum's advice to all her children – '*Put your brain in gear before opening your mouth*' – your words will last a lifetime and could affect a pupil's life forever.

- Teaching is a rewarding job but you need to think outside of the box and dare to be different if you want to be a truly successful educationalist.

- Look for the 'Alice' in your classroom. They may just be asking for a little bit of help and kindness through their body language and behaviours.

Further reading

Taylor, C (2012) *Improving Alternative Provision*. Department for Education. [online] Available at: www.gov.uk/government/publications/improving-alternative-provision (accessed 9 January 2024).

References

Castaneda, C (1998) *The Teachings of Don Juan: A Yaqui Way of Knowledge*. Berkeley, CA: University of California Press.

Children's Commissioner for Wales (2014) *Right to Learn*. Report. Cardiff: Children's Commissioner for Wales.

Fahlberg, V (1994) *A Child's Journey through Placement*. London: Jessica Kingsley Publishers.

Mandela, N (1990) Nelson Mandela Visits Madison Park HS in Roxbury in 1990. GBH News, 24 June. [online] Available at: www.youtube.com/watch?v=b66c6OkMZGw (accessed 9 January 2024).

Reidy, T (2012) Excluded Pupils Find Few Opportunities Outside Mainstream State School. *The Guardian*, 2 December. [online] Available at: www.theguardian.com/education/2012/dec/02/ecluded-pupils-few-chances-outside-school (accessed 9 January 2024).

Index

For Product Safety Concerns and Information please contact our EU
representative GPSR@taylorandfrancis.com
Taylor & Francis Verlag GmbH, Kaufingerstraße 24, 80331 München, Germany

www.ingramcontent.com/pod-product-compliance
Ingram Content Group UK Ltd.
Pitfield, Milton Keynes, MK11 3LW, UK
UKHW030739060925
462614UK00021B/522

* 9 781915 713605 *